Character Education
The Ladder to Success

Grades 4-6

by Leland Graham, Ph.D.
& Isabelle McCoy, M.Ed.

Carson-Dellosa Publishing Company, Inc.
Greensboro, North Carolina

Acknowledgments

The authors gratefully acknowledge the assistance and suggestions of the following persons:
Cynthia Denman, Coco Graham, Thomas McCoy,
Beverly Moody, Dianne Selman, and Connie York.

About the Authors

Dr. Leland Graham is a former teacher, principal, and college professor. During his teaching career, he was twice voted Outstanding Teacher of the Year. Over the years, Leland has presented numerous educational workshops across the U.S. and for NSSEA. He currently works as Marketing Director for The School Box, a chain of school supply stores based in Atlanta. Dr. Graham has written or coauthored more than 45 books for the educational market.

Isabelle McCoy has 29 years of experience teaching grades 4–8. She holds a bachelor's degree in elementary education from the University of Georgia in Athens and a master's degree in education from Georgia State University in Atlanta. Isabelle taught at the elementary level for 22 years, earning a Teacher of the Year award in 1994. For the last seven years, Isabelle has taught social studies at Henderson Middle School. She has served as the Social Studies Department Chairperson for the last two years. Isabelle is married with three sons and one grandson. She has coauthored a total of nine books with Dr. Graham.

Credits

Authors: Leland Graham, Ph.D. and Isabelle McCoy, M.Ed.
Editors: Kelly Morris Huxmann and Karen Seberg
Layout Design: Mark Conrad
Typesetting: Sharon Thompson
Inside Illustrations: Tim Foley
Cover Design: Peggy Jackson
Cover Image: © Photo www.comstock.com and
    © Digital Vision® Ltd. All rights reserved.

Table of Contents

How to Use This Book

Human life is character building; for remember that character means exactly
what we are, while reputation is only what other people think we are.
Every man builds his own character. — Cuyler

Developing a good, strong character is like climbing a ladder—each step brings you closer to your goal. But what exactly do we mean by the word *character*? Character is defined as a combination of qualities or features that makes one person, group, or thing different from another. This book has been written to help you and your students develop nine important character traits: self-discipline, kindness, respect, responsibility, honesty, fairness, courage, perseverance, and citizenship. Once instilled, these key traits and values will help guide your students to make good decisions and achieve success.

Each section of this book begins with a definition of the character trait, followed by a variety of related activities for your students. Follow the tips below and throughout the book for using the pages, or adapt the materials in a way that best suits the needs of your class.

What Is . . . ? — Photocopy the opening page on each character trait for the students or create a transparency to use with the class. Use the definition to begin a discussion of each trait. Ask students to interpret the quotations. Divide the class into small groups to discuss the "Steps to follow . . ." Ask students to share concrete examples of things they can do to follow these steps.

Inspiration Poster — Enlarge and color each inspiration poster to display in your classroom. Alternately, use the page to make a transparency to help lead discussion. Students may also use each poster idea as a springboard for creating their own posters.

Brainstorming — Before handing out the Brainstorming worksheet, lead a class brainstorming session on each trait. Make a transparency of the Brainstorming Graphic Organizer (page 93) and write the trait (e.g., "honesty") in the center oval. Ask students to name the first words that come to mind when they think of that trait. Write these words (e.g., "truthful") along the spokes. Then ask students to name things people could do to demonstrate the trait (e.g., "Tell the truth."). Write these actions on the lines provided. After the brainstorming session, photocopy and distribute the Brainstorming worksheet to students. Allow students time to complete the page in class or at home. Collect all nine completed pages to make small booklets for the students.

Literature Connection — Use each literature selection to reinforce what students are learning about character. Encourage students to identify and discuss how different character traits are represented in the reading. Use the accompanying activities to extend the learning.

Famous Quotations — Photocopy and cut apart the quotations along the dotted lines. Fold the paper strips in half and put them in a box or hat. Have several students select strips from the box and read their quotations aloud. Discuss the meaning of each quotation. Later, distribute copies of the page of quotations to students, or create a transparency to use with the whole class. Ask students to choose one or more of the quotations to write about in their journals.

Critical Thinking — Photocopy and distribute these pages to individual students or small groups. Have students work in small groups to discuss and answer the questions, then bring the groups back together for a full-class discussion.

Bulletin Board Set — Use the ideas as given by enlarging and photocopying the pieces onto heavier paper stock. Use to decorate your classroom and promote discussion.

What Is Self-Discipline?

> **Self-Discipline** . . . is the training and control of one's self and one's conduct, usually for personal improvement. When practicing self-discipline, you agree to live within limits created not only by yourself but also those created by others. Self-discipline is practiced in the way people speak to and act toward one another. In addition, self-discipline applies to the way a person allocates time. On the most basic level, self-discipline mirrors the habits of good living.

Self-reverence, self-knowledge, self-control. Those three alone lead life to sovereign power. — Lord Alfred Tennyson

In the long run, we shape our lives . . . And the choices we make are ultimately our own responsibility. — Eleanor Roosevelt

Steps to follow to show self-discipline:

▶ Exhibit self-control. Make choices that are respectful, kind, and healthy.

▶ Stay on task. Listen to your teacher or parents, and follow directions.

▶ Ignore peer pressure. Do what is right, not what is popular.

▶ Follow school, class, and home rules. Think before you speak or act.

▶ Complete all assignments. Write down what is expected and when the work is due. Take all needed materials home. Set aside a place and time for completing homework and projects.

▶ Set personal and community goals. Select goals that you can achieve. List ways to achieve those goals.

▶ Be productive rather than destructive. Choose activities that will have a positive impact on your life or your community.

Citizenship • Perseverance • Courage • Fairness • Honesty • Responsibility • Respect • Kindness • Self-Discipline

CD-0072 *Character Education*

Inspire your students to practice self-discipline. Enlarge, decorate, and display this poster in your classroom or copy it and make a transparency to use with your class. Ask students to think of other ways they can show self-discipline at school.

Poster Follow-up

 After discussing the "Think Before You Act or Speak!" poster, answer the questions below. Be prepared to explain your answers.

1. Did Kelly demonstrate self-discipline? Explain your answer.

   _____

   _____

   _____

2. Did Amy demonstrate self-discipline? Explain your answer.

   _____

   _____

   _____

3. What do you think was the result of Kelly and Amy's encounter?

   _____

   _____

   _____

4. How could these students have demonstrated self-discipline?

   _____

   _____

   _____

5. If you had been in this situation, what would you have said about Amy's shoes? Does your answer demonstrate self-discipline? Why or why not?

   _____

   _____

   _____

6. Have you ever experienced a similar situation? If so, please explain.

   _____

   _____

   _____

Brainstorming

 Close your eyes and think about the word *self-discipline*. What other words come to mind? If you are stumped, try filling in the blank: "Someone who shows self-discipline is _____." Add your responses to the diagram below. A few words have been given to help you get started.

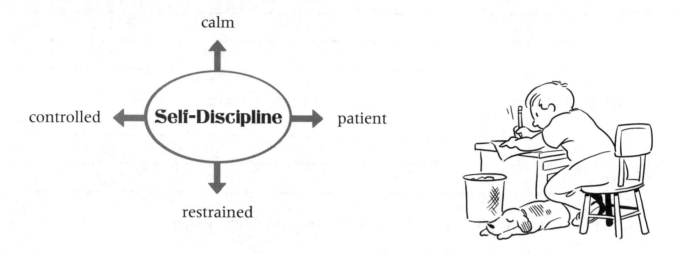

calm

controlled ← **Self-Discipline** → patient

restrained

Look at the words in your diagram. How do they relate to things you have done over the last week or two? On the lines below, try to list three situations in which you showed self-discipline. Then list three situations in which you did NOT show self-discipline. Explain what you could have done differently to show more self-control.

Showed self-discipline	**Did NOT show self-discipline**
1. _____	1. _____
_____	_____
_____	_____
2. _____	2. _____
_____	_____
_____	_____
3. _____	3. _____
_____	_____
_____	_____

Literature Connection

Read *Hatchet* by Gary Paulsen as a class project. In this story, a boy named Brian Robeson plans to fly to Canada to spend time with his father. While en route, the small plane goes down in the Canadian wilderness after the pilot has a heart attack and dies. Brian, a "city boy," must learn to survive in the wilderness even as he suffers with the pain of his parents' divorce and the deep dark secret he is holding. Read on to discover how Brian spends 54 days in the wilderness and learns self-discipline.

Materials

- *Hatchet* by Gary Paulsen
- Notebook or journal
- Pencil or pen
- Cardboard or poster board
- Markers, crayons, or colored pencils
- Scissors
- String or yarn
- 8" (20 cm) dowel
- Paper plate

Creating a Mobile

Create a colorful, eye-catching mobile to display examples of how Brian showed self-discipline while out in the wilderness.

1. In a notebook or journal, list examples from the book *Hatchet* where Brian shows self-discipline.

2. Use cardboard or poster board to create a picture or shape for each item on your list. Neatly write one example of Brian's self-discipline on each picture.

3. Color and cut out each shape or picture.

4. Cut several pieces of string or yarn approximately 18" (46 cm) long.

5. Take one length of string and attach one end to the middle of the dowel. Wrap it around the dowel a few times and secure with a knot. Make a small hole in the center of the paper plate. Thread the free end of the string or yarn through the hole in the paper plate. Pull the string through the hole to draw the dowel tightly against the plate. Tie a knot in the upper end of the string to secure the dowel in place and trim the excess string.

6. Attach the other pieces of string or yarn to the outside rim of the paper plate. Tie a picture to the loose end of each string. Make sure that the pictures are balanced so that your mobile does not lean to one side.

Famous Quotations

 Read the quotations below. Choose one or more and write what you think they mean on a sheet of notebook paper or in your journal. Then give some examples of ways that you can demonstrate self-discipline each day.

I am myself my own commander. — Plautus

Nothing gives one person so much advantage over another as to remain always cool and unruffled under all circumstances. — Thomas Jefferson

He is strong who conquers others; he who conquers himself is mighty. — Lao-tzu

To know one's self is the true; to strive with one's self is the good; to conquer one's self is the beautiful. — Joseph Roux

If you will think about what you ought to do for other people, your character will take care of itself. — Woodrow Wilson

The measure of a man's character is what he would do if he knew he never would be found out. — Thomas Babington Macaulay

Man cannot live without self-control. — Isaac Bashevis Singer

The use of self-control is like the use of brakes on a train. — Bertrand Russell

I count him braver who overcomes his desires than him who conquers his enemies; for the hardest victory is [the victory] over self. — Aristotle

Role-Playing

 Teacher: Divide the class into small groups. Copy and cut apart the role-playing situations below and have each group select a situation to act out. Give the groups 10 minutes to discuss and prepare their presentations.

Following each group's presentation, have the rest of the class describe ways in which the characters could have demonstrated self-discipline. After the class discussion, have the groups incorporate their classmates' suggestions to reenact their situations, this time demonstrating self-discipline.

Ariel steps on LaPorsha's shoes during class change in a crowded hallway.	Coach McCoy does not allow you to play first string on the football team.
Melvin's little brother Joshua borrows Melvin's favorite CD without asking permission. He accidentally breaks it.	Jessica is mad at her best friend and throws her purse across the room.
Your teacher accuses you of talking during a geography test.	Your best friend Juanita gets the part in the school play that you wanted.
Darriel has postponed working on his science project until the day before it is due.	Your mother does not allow you to have snacks before dinner, but she is not home.
Arthur doesn't do his homework and makes up an excuse.	Your friend Jerry sneaks the ice cream from your lunch tray and eats it.

Critical Thinking

Read the story silently or take turns reading aloud in your group. Then work with your group to answer the discussion questions below. Use another sheet of paper if necessary.

Arnita Collins and Maria Sanchez are best friends. Since they live on the same street, their parents are also friends. They have known each other since kindergarten. Both girls are also friends with Caroline Schmidt. Caroline, originally from Baltimore, is new to the school this year.

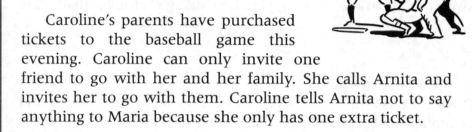

Caroline's parents have purchased tickets to the baseball game this evening. Caroline can only invite one friend to go with her and her family. She calls Arnita and invites her to go with them. Caroline tells Arnita not to say anything to Maria because she only has one extra ticket.

Arnita has a difficult decision to make. On the one hand, she knows how much Maria loves baseball. As a matter of fact, Maria has a mad crush on one of the baseball players. Her bedroom walls are plastered with his pictures. On the other hand, Arnita has never been to a baseball game before because her family really cannot afford it. Arnita must also consider a book report that is due the next day. She has known about this book report for three weeks, but she has not finished it yet. Arnita decides to go to the game anyway.

The next day at school, Mrs. Todd, the English teacher, asks Arnita for her book report. . . .

1. Did Arnita show self-discipline? Explain your answer.

2. What could Arnita have done to demonstrate more self-discipline?

3. What do you think will happen when Maria discovers that Arnita went to the game?

4. What do you think Arnita's parents will do when they find out that she didn't complete her book report on time?

5. What would you have done in Arnita's place?

Bulletin Board Set

Use this bulletin board idea to reinforce the concept of self-discipline in your classroom. Enlarge the pieces below and glue them onto colorful sheets of construction paper, card stock, or poster board. Have students add their own dos and don'ts to the set. Arrange the pieces to create a colorful display.

Materials

▶ Bulletin board pieces below

▶ Markers, pens, or colored pencils

▶ Construction paper, card stock, or poster board

▶ Scissors

▶ School glue

▶ Pushpins or stapler

Do...

Don't...

Control your actions and words.

Let your thoughts and feelings control your actions.

Follow a routine for completing your homework each night.

Procrastinate on completing your assignments or chores.

Stand up for what you believe in and for what is right!

Give in to negative peer pressure.

Treat others as you would like to be treated.

Treat friends or others unkindly.

What Is Kindness?

Kindness . . . is being generous, friendly, or warm-hearted. It means having a kind and gentle nature. Kindness involves doing good rather than harm. When practicing kindness, people show an understanding for others and treat them with respect. Kindness involves doing thoughtful deeds for people who are in need. It often means putting other people's feelings before your own. When people are kind, they feel compassion.

No act of kindness, no matter how small, is ever wasted. — Aesop

What wisdom can you find that is greater than kindness?
— Jean-Jacques Rousseau

Steps to follow to show kindness:

▶ Try to appreciate others' talents and skills.

▶ Comfort and help those who need assistance.

▶ Help those who are less fortunate.

▶ Show consideration and kindness through your actions and words.

▶ Show your appreciation by thanking those who do you a kindness.

▶ Help others because it is right, not because it is required.

▶ Show forgiveness to those who have hurt you.

▶ Put others' needs before your own.

▶ Be a good listener.

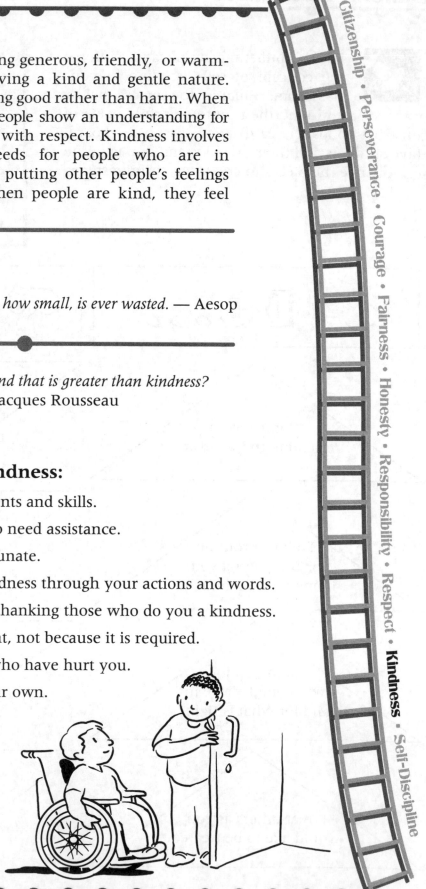

Citizenship • Perseverance • Courage • Fairness • Honesty • Responsibility • Respect • Kindness • Self-Discipline

Inspire your students to practice kindness. Enlarge, decorate, and display this poster in your classroom or copy it and make a transparency to use with your class. Ask students to think of other ways they can show kindness in the community.

Nothing is so popular as

KINDNESS

— Cicero

Ask yourself . . .

How can I help those who are less fortunate?

Poster Follow-up

Name _____

 After discussing the "Nothing is so popular as kindness" poster, answer the questions below. Be prepared to explain your answers.

1. Did the students demonstrate kindness? Give reasons for your answer.

   _____

   _____

   _____

2. What time of year do you think this occurred? Are there other times of the year that this act of kindness could be shown? Explain your answer.

   _____

   _____

   _____

3. Who do you think will benefit from this act of kindness?

   _____

   _____

   _____

4. What are some other ways these students could show kindness?

   _____

   _____

   _____

5. If you were collecting cans of food, what would you say to those who make donations? Why is that important?

   _____

   _____

   _____

6. Have you ever collected donations for the needy? If so, describe how it made you feel.

   _____

   _____

   _____

Brainstorming

 Close your eyes and think about the word *kindness*. What other words come to mind? If you are stumped, try filling in the blank: "Someone who shows kindness is _____." Add your responses to the diagram below. A few words have been given to help you get started.

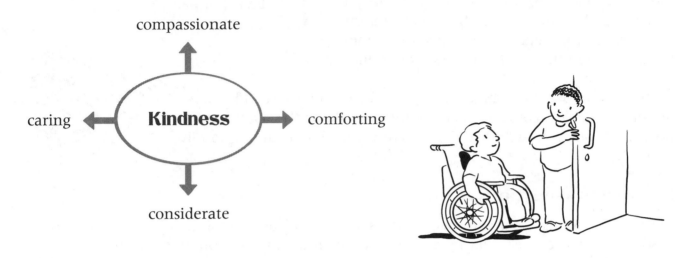

Look at the words in your diagram. How do they relate to things you have done over the last week or two? On the lines below, try to list three situations in which you showed kindness. Then list three situations in which you did NOT show kindness. Explain what you could have done differently to be more kind.

Showed kindness	**Did NOT show kindness**
1. _____ _____ _____	1. _____ _____ _____
2. _____ _____ _____	2. _____ _____ _____
3. _____ _____ _____	3. _____ _____ _____

Literature Connection

 Read *Charlie and the Chocolate Factory* by Roald Dahl as a class project. The main character, Charlie Bucket, and his family are extremely poor. As a matter of fact, the family hardly has enough money to buy food. Mr. Bucket loses his job and things become worse. Each year for his birthday, Charlie receives one chocolate candy bar. It is one of the few happinesses in his life.

Materials

▶ *Charlie and the Chocolate Factory* by Roald Dahl
▶ Notebook paper or journal
▶ Pencil or pen

Willie Wonka owns the largest chocolate factory in the world and decides to have a contest. Read on to learn about the contest and how Mr. Wonka shows great kindness towards Charlie and his family.

Discussion Questions

Working in groups of three to five students, choose at least two of the following questions to discuss. Choose a recorder to take notes on your discussion. You must include evidence from the book to support your answers. After time is given for discussion (approximately 10 minutes), choose one of your group members to be the reporter. The reporter will share your answers with the class.

1. Why can't Charlie's family afford to buy a larger house or enough food to eat?

    _____

2. If you could be friends with any of the children who found golden tickets, which one would you choose? Why?

    _____

    _____

3. Why did the family choose Grandpa Joe to go with Charlie to the chocolate factory?

    _____

4. Why is Charlie so well behaved during the tour of the factory? Explain.

    _____

    _____

5. How does Willie Wonka demonstrate kindness? Explain.

    _____

    _____

Famous Quotations

 Read the quotations below. Choose one or more and write what you think they mean on a sheet of notebook paper or in your journal. Then give some examples of ways that you can demonstrate kindness each day.

People must help one another; it is nature's law. — Jean de La Fontaine

Kindness begets kindness. — Proverb

One kind action is better than a thousand kind thoughts. — Unknown

Kindness in words creates confidence. Kindness in thinking creates profoundness. Kindness in giving creates love. — Lao-tzu

Men are only as great as they are kind. — Elbert Hubbard

Kindness is the sunshine in which virtue grows. — R. G. Ingersoll

Kindness consists in loving people more than they deserve. — Joseph Joubert

Good Will is the mightiest practical force in the universe. — Charles Fletcher Dole

To be able to practice five things everywhere under heaven constitutes perfect virtue. [They are] gravity, generosity of soul, sincerity, earnestness, and kindness. — Confucius

Nothing is so popular as kindness. — Cicero

Practicing Kindness

Teacher: Use the following activities to explore kindness in your classroom.

Kids Being Kind

Declare one week "Kindness Week." On Monday, have all the students in your class write their names on slips of paper. Put the slips of paper in a bowl or basket. Then ask each student to draw a name from the bowl. The person whose name is drawn is the student's "Kids Being Kind" partner. Ask students not to tell anyone whose names they drew. Throughout Kindness Week, students are to do at least one kind deed each day for their partners. These kind acts can be obvious, such as putting a treat or cheery note on a partner's desk, or they can be more subtle. At the end of the week, have students reveal the names of their "Kids Being Kind" partners and describe their kind deeds. You may want to ask students to keep a log of their acts of kindness in a notebook or journal.

Thanks for Your Kindness Note

Ask students to think of something kind that someone has done for them. It could have been something small, such as holding a door open, picking up something that they dropped, or lending them some change. Showing and expressing thanks for a kind deed is a way of showing kindness in return. Photocopy the card below. Have each student write a thank-you note to someone for being kind. Remind students to mention the reason that they are thanking the person in their notes.

THANK YOU

Critical Thinking

Name _____

 Read the passage about Jane Addams. Read silently or take turns reading aloud in your group. Then work with your group to answer the discussion questions below.

More than one hundred years ago, Jane Addams, an American-born woman, devoted her life to helping the poor. When Jane was a young woman, she visited Europe and learned about a program where educated young men lived in a poor section of London and taught classes to the people in their neighborhood. She liked this idea so much that when she returned to her home in Chicago, she started Hull House in 1889.

Jane Addams and her friends used a huge mansion located in an area where poor immigrants lived to start a program of classes similar to the one in London. They taught job skills, started a kindergarten, cared for the children of the immigrants, and began a boys' club called the Young Heroes Club. Through the kind acts of Jane Addams and her friends, the people in this neighborhood were able to find food, financial help, and friendship at Hull House.

1. Where did Jane Addams get the idea for Hull House?

   _____

   _____

2. In what ways did Jane and her friends demonstrate kindness?

   _____

   _____

3. How would an immigrant living in Chicago in the 1880s have benefited from Hull House?

   _____

   _____

4. Are there places or people in your hometown who perform similarly kind deeds? List them and describe the type of work they do.

   _____

   _____

   _____

Bulletin Board Set

Use this bulletin board idea to reinforce the concept of kindness in your classroom. Enlarge and color the pieces below, then glue them onto colorful sheets of construction paper, card stock, or poster board. Have students add their own examples of kind acts using pictures and/or words. (They may include examples from their "Kindness Week" logs.) Arrange the pieces to create a colorful display.

Materials

▶ Bulletin board pieces below
▶ Markers, pens, or colored pencils
▶ Construction paper, card stock, or poster board
▶ Scissors
▶ School glue
▶ Pushpins or stapler

What Is Respect?

> **Respect** . . . is concern for the rights of others. It also means treating others as you would want them to treat you. In other words, showing respect means following the Golden Rule. Respect is also understanding that even though people have differences, they also have similar feelings and needs. In order to demonstrate respect, you must use good manners, be polite, show consideration, and value the property of other people. If you treat others with courtesy, you are being respectful.

We must each respect others even as we respect ourselves. — U Thant

───────────●───────────

No one is happy unless he respects himself. — Jean-Jacques Rousseau

Steps to follow to show respect:

▶ Follow the Golden Rule—that is, treat others as you would like to be treated.

▶ Use good manners.

▶ Show consideration for other people's feelings.

▶ Treat others with kindness and caring.

▶ Recognize and appreciate the value of people, property, the environment, and yourself.

▶ Accept others' differences.

▶ Respond peacefully to anger and insults.

▶ Respect all living and nonliving things.

▶ Value cultural diversity.

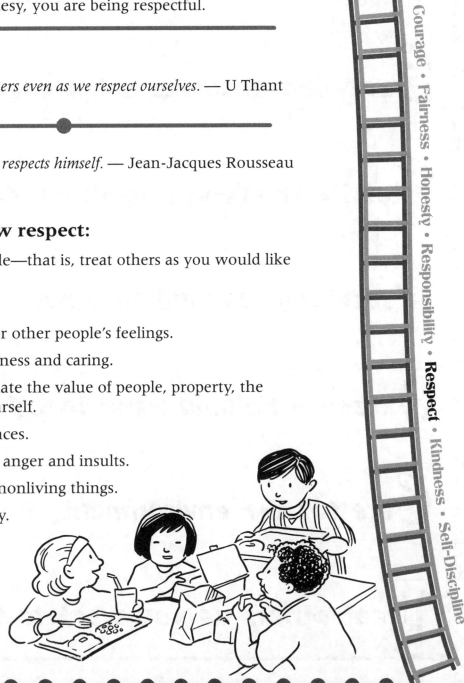

Citizenship • Perseverance • Courage • Fairness • Honesty • Responsibility • **Respect** • Kindness • Self-Discipline

Inspire your students to practice respect. Enlarge, decorate, and display this poster in your classroom or copy it and make a transparency to use with your class. Ask students to name other ways they can show respect each day.

Raise your hand to speak in class.

Everyone deserves a fair chance.

Send a thank-you to those deserving.

Peacefully respond to others' anger.

Extend a helping hand to others.

Care for the environment.

Treat others as you want to be treated.

Exploring Respect

Your teacher will divide the class into small groups. Each group will select one of the writing activities below. Work together to complete the activity in the space provided. (Use additional paper if necessary.) Be prepared to share your work with the rest of the class.

1. Take each letter of the word *respect* and write your own acrostic poem, similar to the one found on the "R E S P E C T" poster.

2. Make a list of school staff members (excluding teachers), such as a nurse, secretary, custodian, or cafeteria worker. Choose someone from the list and write a letter explaining why you appreciate that person's work. Be sure to mention ways that respect relates to the staff member's position.

3. Write a letter to a person in a nursing home. Ask for advice on how to be a respectful person. Tell the senior citizen your plans for the future and describe how you might demonstrate respect.

4. Describe 5 to 10 ways that demonstrate how you can show respect at home, at school, and in the community.

_____

_____

_____

_____

_____

_____

_____

_____

_____

_____

_____

Brainstorming

 Close your eyes and think about the word *respect*. What other words come to mind? If you are stumped, try filling in the blank: "Someone who shows respect is _____." Add your responses to the diagram below. A few words have been given to help you get started.

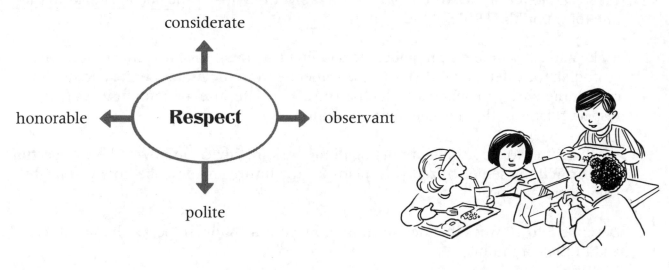

considerate

honorable ← **Respect** → observant

polite

Look at the words in your diagram. How do they relate to things you have done over the last week or two? On the lines below, try to list three situations in which you showed respect. Then list three situations in which you did NOT show respect. Explain what you could have done differently to be more respectful.

Showed respect	**Did NOT show respect**
1. _____	1. _____
_____	_____
_____	_____
2. _____	2. _____
_____	_____
_____	_____
3. _____	3. _____
_____	_____
_____	_____

Literature Connection

Respect

Read *Number the Stars* by Lois Lowry as a class project. In the story, Ellen Rosen and her best friend, Annemarie Johansen, are returning home from school when they are stopped on the corner by German soldiers. The girls do not realize that soldiers on the street corners and rationed food are only the beginning of the problems they will face under Denmark's occupation by the Nazis. Annemarie and her family are Protestant, but Ellen's family is Jewish. The Rosen family discovers that they are to be relocated. They decide to escape. Read on to learn how Annemarie takes part in saving Ellen's life.

Materials

▶ *Number the Stars* by Lois Lowry
▶ Notebook paper or journal
▶ Pencil or pen

Writing a Found Poem

A "found poem" is a collection of key words or phrases quoted from other sources. Here is an example of a found poem using phrases from *Number the Stars*:

> "Nazis, enormous enemy"
> "There has been a death . . ."
> " . . . pretend to be a silly, empty-headed little girl."

When you put these words or phrases from the text together, they form a found poem. The poem should allow you to return to the story to focus on those vivid words or phrases used by the author. On a sheet of paper, list several key words or phrases from *Number the Stars*. These words or phrases should be ones that stand out in your mind. Put them together to form your own found poem.

Respond to Your Reading!

After reading *Number the Stars*, choose one of the following questions to answer on a separate sheet of paper. Be prepared to share your answers with the class.

1. How will Ellen remember Annemarie and her family when she is older? How will her feelings about the Johansen family compare to her feelings about the German soldiers?

2. Why did some non-Jewish families want to help Jewish families while others did not seem to care? Why were some young men and women like Peter willing to risk their lives to save Jews while fighting the Nazis?

3. What did Annemarie's experiences help her discover about courage, pride, respect, and friendship?

Famous Quotations

 Read the quotations below. Choose one or more and write what you think they mean on a sheet of notebook paper or in your journal. Then give some examples of ways that you can demonstrate respect each day.

Respect yourself most of all. — Pythagoras

I must respect the opinion of others even if I disagree with them.
— Herbert Henry Lehman

Respect others if you want to be respected. — Proverb

You should respect each other and refrain from disputes. — Buddha

Men are respectable only as they respect. — Ralph Waldo Emerson

Never look down on anybody unless you're helping him up. — Jesse Jackson

There is overwhelming evidence that the higher the level of self-esteem, the more likely one will be to treat others with respect, kindness, and generosity. — Nathaniel Branden

If you lead through fear, you will have little to respect; but if you lead through respect, you will have little to fear. — Anonymous

We must all learn to live as brothers, or we will all perish as fools.
— Martin Luther King, Jr.

Practicing Respect

Teacher: Have your students choose one of the following activities on respect.

The Ugly Duckling

Discuss the meaning of the word *tolerance*. How can people show tolerance? Why is this an example of respect? Read the story "The Ugly Duckling" by Hans Christian Andersen. Have the students discuss how the Ugly Duckling was treated. Then have the students rewrite the story to show how the Ugly Duckling could have been treated with respect. Have students share their stories with the class. Ask the students if they can think of any other famous stories (such as "Cinderella") that deal with tolerance and respect.

Role-Playing

Choose one or more of the following situations to role-play. Students may role-play each situation either showing respect or being disrespectful. After each role-playing situation, have the class decide which way was demonstrated.

1. Your father is talking on the phone and you want to ask him a question.

2. You see a student in a wheelchair trying to open the door to the school.

3. You would like more macaroni and cheese, but it is at the end of the table.

4. You and your little brother want to listen to different kinds of music.

It's Not Easy Being Green

Locate a copy of the song "It's Not Easy Being Green" sung by Kermit the Frog. Play the song for the class. Divide the class into groups of three or four students to discuss what it means to be different and how it feels. You may want to give students a few sample questions to get them started: *Are you short or tall? Do you wear glasses? Is there someone in your class or school with a physical disability? Are there students from other countries or cultures? What are ways to demonstrate respect for those who are different than you?*

Critical Thinking

Name _____

Read the passage about Eleanor Roosevelt, nicknamed the "First Lady of the World." Read silently or take turns reading aloud in your group. Then work with your group to answer the discussion questions below.

Eleanor Roosevelt was born on October 11, 1884 in New York City. As a child she was shy, afraid, lonely, and sad. As an adult, however, she put aside her own insecurities to champion the cause of equality and respect for all. Eleanor Roosevelt was the wife of President Franklin D. Roosevelt, also known as FDR. Mrs. Roosevelt sincerely believed in the right to "life, liberty, and the pursuit of happiness." These words were stated in the United States' Declaration of Independence.

In 1939, Marian Anderson, an African-American opera singer, was scheduled to perform at Constitution Hall in Washington, D.C. Miss Anderson is said to have had one of the finest voices of all times. However, some of the members of the Daughters of the American Revolution (DAR) did not want a black person singing in their auditorium. Her performance was canceled. Mrs. Roosevelt, a member of the DAR, was outraged. She resigned from the DAR and arranged for Miss Anderson to perform at the Lincoln Memorial instead. Seventy-five thousand people came to listen to her sing on Easter Sunday of 1939.

Eleanor Roosevelt's life demonstrated her commitment to fighting for respect for all people as well as against racial injustice. She worked for social reforms and became known as the "First Lady of the World."

No one can make you feel inferior without your consent.
— Eleanor Roosevelt

1. How did Eleanor Roosevelt show respect for others?

   _____

   _____

2. Do you think Mrs. Roosevelt was justified in resigning from the DAR? Why or why not?

   _____

   _____

3. The Declaration of Independence states that all men are created equal and have equal rights. How do you think Eleanor Roosevelt tried to make these words a reality?

   _____

   _____

Use this bulletin board idea to reinforce the concept of respect in your classroom. Enlarge and color the pieces below, then glue them onto colorful sheets of construction paper, card stock, or poster board. Have students think of other examples of respectful behavior and draw pictures to add to the set. Arrange the pieces to create a colorful display.

Materials

▶ Bulletin board pieces below

▶ Markers, pens, or colored pencils

▶ Construction paper, card stock, or poster board

▶ Scissors

▶ School glue

▶ Pushpins or stapler

Ways to Show Respect

to others . . .

to the environment . . .

to yourself . . .

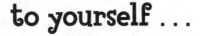

Say NO to Drugs!

What Is Responsibility?

Responsibility . . . means being accountable for who you are and what you do. Responsibility is being dependable and trustworthy. Someone who is responsible does her best and doesn't blame others for her mistakes. A responsible person makes sure a job is done correctly and on time. A person who is responsible has a moral duty to follow through and complete a task. Trying your best and working hard to complete assigned tasks shows that you are responsible.

A man who enjoys responsibility usually gets it.
— Malcolm Forbes

When you blame others, you give up your power to change.
— Anonymous

Steps to follow to show responsibility:

▶ Find out what needs to be done and do it.

▶ Complete a task without being asked.

▶ Understand and accept the consequences of your actions.

▶ Think before you act.

▶ Do your best.

▶ Clean up after yourself even if no one is watching.

▶ Always try to do the right thing.

▶ Follow through and don't give up.

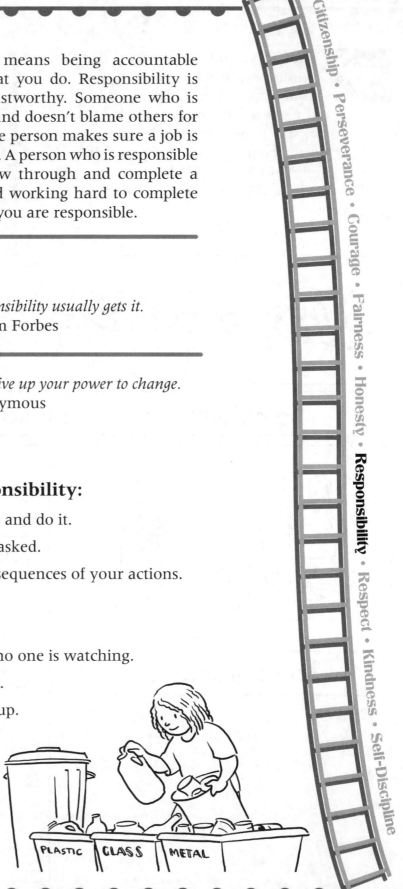

Inspire your students to be responsible. Enlarge, decorate, and display this poster in your classroom or copy it and make a transparency to use with your class. Ask students to name other ways they can show responsibility at home or at school.

Who Is Being Responsible?

At home

At school

In the community

Who's Responsible?

Name _____

Read each situation below. Do the students demonstrate responsible behavior? On the lines provided, explain how the students are showing responsibility. If they are not, explain what the students could have done instead to act more responsibly.

1. Jeffrey is watching his favorite game show when he suddenly remembers that his social studies research paper is due tomorrow. He has not even started it.

   _____

   _____

   _____

2. Mary was tired and went to bed early. She soon realized that she had not emptied the dishwasher as her mother had requested. She got out of bed and completed her chore.

   _____

   _____

   _____

3. While skating in the kitchen, Alicia realized she was leaving black marks on the tile. After unsuccessfully trying to clean the floor, she gave up and went to play basketball.

   _____

   _____

   _____

4. Jamie's little brother is sick. Jamie's mother asks him to watch his brother while she runs an errand. Jamie calls his friend to tell him he cannot go to the ballpark.

   _____

   _____

   _____

5. Richard returned several library books on time. However, he did not tell the librarian that he had accidentally torn a few pages in one of the books on magnets.

   _____

   _____

   _____

Brainstorming

 Close your eyes and think about the word *responsibility*. What other words come to mind? If you are stumped, try filling in the blank: "Someone who shows responsibility is _____." Add your responses to the diagram below. A few words have been given to help you get started.

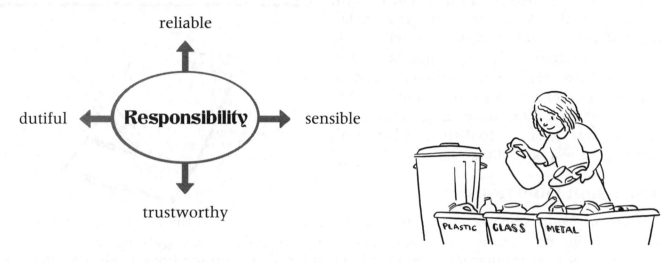

Look at the words in your diagram. How do they relate to things you have done over the last week or two? On the lines below, try to list three situations in which you acted responsibly. Then list three situations in which you did NOT act responsibly. Explain what you could have done differently to be more responsible.

Acted responsibly	Did NOT act responsibly
1. _____	1. _____
_____	_____
_____	_____
2. _____	2. _____
_____	_____
_____	_____
3. _____	3. _____
_____	_____
_____	_____

Literature Connection

Read *Dear Mr. Henshaw* by Beverly Cleary as a class project. When Leigh Botts was in second grade, he became interested in writing to an author named Mr. Henshaw. He continued to write to Mr. Henshaw in third, fourth, fifth, and sixth grades. While in sixth grade, Leigh was assigned a project about an author. He sent Mr. Henshaw a list of 10 questions. Mr. Henshaw answered his questions and sent Leigh a set of questions to answer in return. Mrs. Botts, Leigh's mother, makes Leigh respond to the questions. Read on to discover what Leigh learns about responsibility.

Materials

▶ *Dear Mr. Henshaw* by Beverly Cleary
▶ Notebook paper or journal
▶ Pencil or pen

Discussion Questions

Working in groups of three to five students, choose at least two of the following questions to discuss. Choose a recorder to take notes on your discussion. Include evidence from the book to support your answers. After time is given for discussion (approximately 10 minutes), choose one of your group members to be the reporter. The reporter will share your answers with the class.

1. In what ways did Leigh act irresponsibly? Explain.

   _____

   _____

2. How did Leigh take responsibility for discovering who was stealing his lunch? Explain.

   _____

   _____

3. Is Leigh's father a responsible person? Why or why not?

   _____

   _____

4. How did other students benefit from Leigh's invention? Explain.

   _____

   _____

Famous Quotations

 Read the quotations below. Choose one or more and write what you think they mean on a sheet of notebook paper or in your journal. Then give some examples of ways that you can demonstrate responsibility each day.

We have the Bill of Rights. What we need is a Bill of Responsibilities. — Bill Maher

You cannot escape the responsibility of tomorrow by evading it today.
— Abraham Lincoln

Liberty means responsibility. That is why most men dread it. — George Bernard Shaw

Few things help an individual more than to place responsibility upon him, and to let him know that you trust him. — Booker T. Washington

I am responsible for doing the work I need to do today even though it may be very hard. — Helen Keller

The price of greatness is responsibility. — Sir Winston Churchill

I believe that every right implies a responsibility; every opportunity, an obligation; every possession, a duty. — John D. Rockefeller, Jr.

I cannot do everything, but I can do something. And because I cannot do everything, I will not refuse to do what I can. — Edward Everett Hale

People may fail many times, but they become failures only when they begin to blame someone else. — Anonymous

As you make your bed, so you must lie on it. — Proverb

The buck stops here. — Author unknown

Interview

Before starting on this activity, review the meaning of responsibility. Then choose at least two individuals in your school, home, or community to interview. You may want to consider the school principal, the school secretary, a bus driver, your parents, neighbors, a police officer, a firefighter, a religious leader, a store owner, a doctor, or a paramedic. Add your own questions to the list below and use these questions to frame your interviews. Find out what types of responsibilities are involved in each person's position. In addition, find out what consequences might occur if the person does not meet those responsibilities. If the person gives you permission, take a picture to put in your report. Be sure to thank each person you interviewed either verbally or in writing. Upon completing your interview, write your report using the responses from the questions below. Plan to share your findings with the class.

Materials

▶ Notebook

▶ Interview questions

▶ Pencil or pen

▶ Camera

1. What is your position?

2. How long have you been at this position?

3. What are some of the responsibilities of your position?

4. What consequences are there if you do not meet your responsibilities?

5. Are there any other people who depend on you? If so, explain.

_____

_____

_____

_____

_____

_____

Poetry Connection

Working with a partner, take turns reading the poems about responsibility. After you have read the two poems, make a Venn diagram comparing and contrasting how the character trait of responsibility is shown in each one.

It's Up to You

One song can spark a moment,
One flower can wake the dream.
One tree can start a forest,
One bird can herald spring.

One smile begins a friendship,
One handclasp lifts a soul.
One star can guide a ship at sea,
One word can frame the goal.

One vote can change a nation,
One sunbeam lights a room.
One candle wipes out darkness,
One laugh will conquer gloom.

One step must start each journey,
One word must start each prayer.
One hope will raise our spirits,
One touch can show you care.

One voice can speak with wisdom,
One heart can know what's true.
One life can make the difference,
You see, IT'S UP TO YOU!

— Anonymous

Mr. Nobody

I know a funny little man,
    As quiet as a mouse,
Who does the mischief that is done
    In everybody's house!
There's no one ever sees his face,
    And yet we all agree
That every plate we break was cracked
    By Mr. Nobody.

'Tis he who always tears our books,
    Who leaves the door ajar;
He pulls the buttons from our shirts,
    And scatters pins afar.
That squeaking door will always squeak
    For, prithee, don't you see?
We leave the oiling to be done
    By Mr. Nobody.

He puts damp wood upon the fire,
    That kettles cannot boil;
His are the feet that bring in mud,
    And all the carpets soil.
The papers always are mislaid,
    Who had them last but he?
There's not one tosses them about
    But Mr. Nobody.

The finger-marks upon the door
    By none of us are made;
We never leave the blinds unclosed
    To let the curtains fade.
The ink we never spill; the boots
    That lying 'round you see
Are not our boots—they all belong
    To Mr. Nobody.

— Anonymous

Use this bulletin board idea to reinforce the concept of responsibility in your classroom. Enlarge the pieces below, then glue or trace them onto colorful sheets of construction paper, card stock, or poster board. Cut out extra geometric shapes in different colors. Have students create pictures that show ways to be responsible and glue each picture onto a different shape. Arrange the pieces to create a colorful display.

Materials

▌ Bulletin board pieces below

▌ Markers, pens, or colored pencils

▌ Construction paper, card stock, or poster board

▌ Scissors

▌ School glue

▌ Pushpins or stapler

Shape Up and become More Responsible

What Is Honesty?

Honesty . . . means being truthful, genuine, sincere, trustworthy, loyal, fair, and upright. An honest person tells the truth and does not lie, cheat, or steal. An honest person does not hide anything. A person who is honest is frank and straightforward. Miguel de Cervantes is often quoted as having said, "Honesty is the best policy." This statement explains that it is important to be truthful and to never cheat or steal. If you are honest, your character will always shine through.

If you tell the truth, you don't have to remember anything.
— Mark Twain

Truth stands when everything else falls.
— Proverb

Steps to follow to show honesty:

▶ At home, at school, or in the community, do your best to tell the truth.

▶ Keep your promises.

▶ Express yourself positively.

▶ Tell the truth, regardless of the consequences.

▶ Voice your opinion in a thoughtful manner.

▶ Follow the rules.

▶ Complete assigned tasks and chores.

▶ Avoid telling lies.

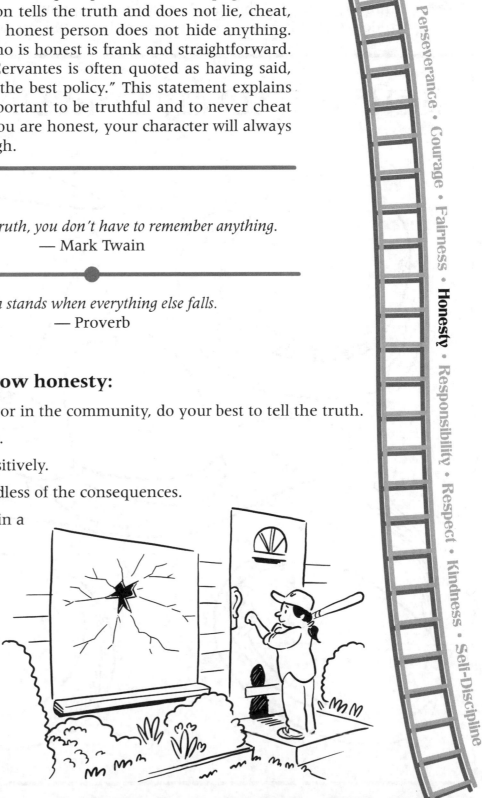

Citizenship • Perseverance • Courage • Fairness • Honesty • Responsibility • Respect • Kindness • Self-Discipline

Inspire your students to practice honesty. Enlarge, decorate, and display this poster in your classroom or copy it and make a transparency to use with your class. Write a phrase (e.g., "Tell the truth" or "Keep your promises") on each hat to remind students what it means to be honest, or have students add the phrases themselves.

Hats off to an honest person!

Evaluating Honesty

Read the situations below dealing with honesty. Answer each question in the space provided.

> During a math test, you look at your friend's paper and copy some of her answers. While grading the papers, the teacher notices that you and your friend missed the same math problems. The teacher questions you about the situation the next day in class.

1. What might happen if your friend is accused of cheating?

   _____

2. If your friend is accused, will you feel guilty? Why or why not?

   _____

3. What might happen if the teacher finds out that you cheated?

   _____

4. What do you think is the best solution to this situation? Explain your answer.

   _____

   _____

> Brandon, a highly ranked tennis player, is preparing to play in the final tournament of the year. In order to keep from getting bumped from his position and losing to a player of lesser rank, Coach Walker suggests to Brandon that he tell the officials he is sick and cannot play in the tournament.

5. If Brandon follows the coach's suggestion, is he being honest or dishonest? Explain your answer.

   _____

   _____

6. Even though there is a chance Brandon will lose, why is it important that he play?

   _____

   _____

7. If you were in this situation, what would you do? Why?

   _____

   _____

Brainstorming

 Close your eyes and think about the word *honesty*. What other words come to mind? If you are stumped, try filling in the blank: "Someone who shows honesty is _____." Add your responses to the diagram below. A few words have been given to help you get started.

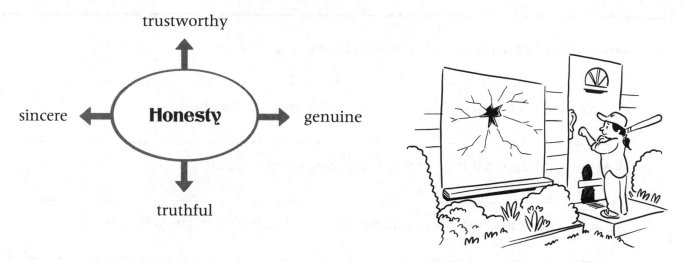

trustworthy

sincere ← **Honesty** → genuine

truthful

Look at the words in your diagram. How do they relate to things you have done over the last week or two? On the lines below, try to list three situations in which you were honest. Then list three situations in which you were NOT honest. Explain what you could have done differently to be more truthful.

Showed honesty

1. _____

_____

_____

2. _____

_____

_____

3. _____

_____

_____

Did NOT show honesty

1. _____

_____

_____

2. _____

_____

_____

3. _____

_____

_____

Literature Connection

 Read *Shiloh* by Phyllis Reynolds Naylor as a class project. In this story, set in Friendly, West Virginia, the main character, Marty Preston, deals with a variety of ethical questions. Marty finds a stray beagle named Shiloh and has difficulty with the ideas of right and wrong, truth and lies, and good and evil. Marty is sure that Shiloh is being abused by Judd Travers, the dog's owner. Marty wants to keep the dog at all costs, and his love for Shiloh grows stronger each day. Since his family is extremely poor and needs to use their money for food, they do not want any pets. Read on to learn how Marty deals with his problems with honesty.

Materials

▶ *Shiloh* by Phyllis Reynolds Naylor
▶ Notebook paper or journal
▶ Pencil or pen

Lies, Lies

In the book *Shiloh*, Marty Preston wrestles with honesty. Even though he knows that lying is wrong, when it comes to protecting Shiloh, Marty is not sure what to do. On the lines provided, write one lie that Marty tells to each of the characters below. Briefly explain why Marty tells each lie and describe the consequences of the lie. Discuss your answers with a partner.

1. Judd Travers _____

_____

_____

2. Marty's mother _____

_____

_____

3. Marty's father _____

_____

_____

4. Dara Lynn _____

_____

_____

5. David Howard _____

_____

_____

Famous Quotations

Read the quotations below. Choose one or more and write what you think they mean on a sheet of notebook paper or in your journal. Then give some examples of ways that you can demonstrate honesty each day.

When in doubt, tell the truth. — Mark Twain

Be true to your work, your word, and your friend. — Henry David Thoreau

A half-truth is a whole lie. — Proverb

A lie has speed but truth has endurance. — Edgar J. Mohn

The truth is more important than the facts. — Frank Lloyd Wright

A truth that's told with bad intent beats all the lies you can invent. — William Blake

A lie stands on one leg, the truth on two. — Benjamin Franklin

Honesty is the first chapter of the book of wisdom. — Thomas Jefferson

The pursuit of truth will set you free—even if you never catch up with it. — Clarence Darrow

Do not do what you would undo if caught. — Leah Arendt

A lie comes back sooner or later. — Proverb

One falsehood spoils a thousand truths. — Proverb

Exploring Honesty

Teacher: Use the following activities to explore honesty in your classroom.

Honesty/Dishonesty Journal

Have students keep an Honesty/Dishonesty Journal for one week. In their journals, have students record events dealing with honesty or dishonesty that they observe throughout the week. Ask them to keep a tally of all the times they hear or tell a "little white lie." In addition to their personal lives, ask students to keep a record of any news stories they see in the papers or on television that deal with honesty. Students may also want to observe television sitcoms. Have them keep track of how often the shows deal with the subject of honesty. At the end of the week, ask students to present their conclusions and share them with the class.

One Lie Leads to Another

Divide students into groups of three or four. Ask each group to think of one positive classroom action, such as completing their own class work. Have the students list several positive effects of doing their own work. Have them write each effect on a separate strip of colored paper, then glue the ends of the strips together to make a paper chain. Next, have students think of the opposite classroom action, such as copying someone else's class work. This time, ask students to list the negative consequences. Have each group make a second paper chain with the negative consequences.

You Be the Judge: Honest or Dishonest

Have students write the words **HONEST** and **DISHONEST** on separate index cards. As you read each of the following statements, ask students to decide whether the situation shows someone behaving honestly or dishonestly. Have students hold up the appropriate card.

▶ Jerome leaves his lunch money sitting on his desk. Frederick takes the money when Jerome is not looking.

▶ Your friend Ana offers to give you a piece of candy if you let her see your homework.

▶ As you are walking home from school, you find an expensive watch with your neighbor's name engraved on it. You decide to leave the watch where you found it.

Critical Thinking

Read the passage about Sitting Bull. Read silently or take turns reading aloud in your group. Then work with your group to answer the discussion questions below.

Sitting Bull, a famous medicine man and leader of the Hunkpapa Sioux, was the main medicine man involved in the Battle of Little Bighorn. He was born about 1831 in what is now South Dakota. After he showed great bravery in a fight, his father gave him the name Sitting Bull. He developed a reputation as a generous, sincere, honest, and wise man. Sitting Bull was devoted to his people and his family. He earned respect among Native Americans and whites alike for being a natural leader and for his generosity and friendliness.

It has been said that Sitting Bull never broke a treaty with the United States government. Many army officers had trusting relationships with him. Sitting Bull also kept his promises to his own people when he promised to lead them and to protect them and their way of life. When the white settlers decided they wanted Native American land, however, they broke their treaties.

1. List several ways that Sitting Bull demonstrated the trait of honesty.

    _____

    _____

    _____

2. Do you think it was difficult for Sitting Bull to keep his promises both to his people and to the white settlers? Explain.

    _____

    _____

    _____

3. Why do you think the U.S. government broke its treaties with the Native Americans?

    _____

    _____

    _____

Bulletin Board Set

 Use this bulletin board idea to reinforce the concept of honesty in your classroom. Enlarge the pieces below, making one silhouette for every student. Cut out and glue the pieces onto colorful sheets of construction paper, card stock, or poster board. Have students write different ways to show honesty on the silhouettes. Arrange the pieces to create a colorful display.

Materials

- Bulletin board pieces below
- Markers, pens, or colored pencils
- Construction paper, card stock, or poster board
- Scissors
- School glue
- Pushpins or stapler

A FEW HONEST STUDENTS

What Is Fairness?

Fairness . . . means being impartial, just, or free of favoritism. It means treating everyone the same. Someone who is fair values equality and is willing to correct his mistakes. If you follow the rules and are honest and reasonable, you are demonstrating fairness. Sometimes it may be difficult for you to understand fairness, but it is important to learn how to treat people equally. When you make sure that others are not treated badly and you do what is right, you are being fair.

Fair play's a jewel. — Proverb

It is not fair to ask of others what you are unwilling to do yourself.
— Eleanor Roosevelt

Steps to follow to show fairness:

▶ Treat people equally.

▶ Share with others.

▶ Listen to what others have to say.

▶ Play by the rules.

▶ Give others the respect, time, and energy that they deserve.

▶ Be open-minded.

▶ Treat those with disabilities fairly.

▶ Do not take advantage of others.

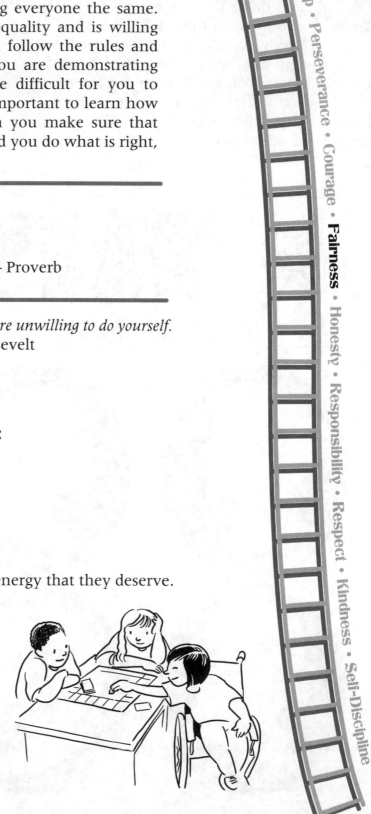

Citizenship · Perseverance · Courage · **Fairness** · Honesty · Responsibility · Respect · Kindness · Self-Discipline

Inspiration Poster

Inspire your students to practice fairness. Enlarge, decorate, and display this poster in your classroom or copy it and make a transparency to use with your class. Ask students to name different ways they can show fairness at school and at home.

The sun shines upon all alike!

– Proverb

Exploring Fairness

Teacher: Use the following activities to explore fairness in your classroom.

Let's Vote

Arrange for your class to vote on a simple topic. What should the school's new mascot be—a tiger or an eagle? Where should the class go on their next field trip—to the museum or to the planetarium? What should the class snack be—chocolate chip cookies or brownies?

Next, give half the class red tokens and the other half green tokens. Label two containers each with one of the choices. The students will vote by placing their tokens in the container of their choice.

> ◗ Tally the number of tokens for each choice and write the results on the board.

> ◗ Now tell the students that only the green tokens count. Count again, tallying only the green tokens, and write the results on the board.

> ◗ Discuss with the class the fairness of this vote.

Explain that at one time in the United States, only property owners could vote. For many years, women and African Americans were not allowed to vote either. Ask the students, "Was this fair? How would you feel if this happened to you?"

Pictures of Unfairness

Look at newspapers, magazines, the Internet, and other sources to find three or more pictures that show unfairness. These pictures may show images of poverty, discrimination, violence, or other injustices. Photocopy, cut, or print out the images and place them around the classroom. Give each student three or more self-stick notes. Tell the students to study each picture and write one sentence on a note describing their feelings about that picture. Have the students post their notes beside the pictures. Allow students time to read what the others have written. Hold a class discussion related to their comments.

Brainstorming

 Close your eyes and think about the word *fairness*. What other words come to mind? If you are stumped, try filling in the blank: "Someone who demonstrates fairness is _____." Add your responses to the diagram below. A few words have been given to help you get started.

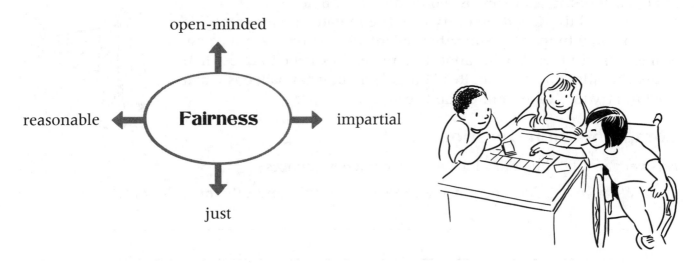

Look at the words in your diagram. How do they relate to things you have done over the last week or two? On the lines below, try to list three situations in which you showed fairness. Then list three situations in which you did NOT show fairness. Explain what you could have done differently to be more fair.

Showed fairness	**Did NOT show fairness**
1. _____	1. _____
_____	_____
_____	_____
2. _____	2. _____
_____	_____
_____	_____
3. _____	3. _____
_____	_____
_____	_____

Literature Connection

Fairness

Read *Holes* by Louis Sachar as a class project. Stanley Yelnats, the main character, is under a curse that began with his great-great-grandfather. He has been unjustly accused and imprisoned in a boys' detention center called Camp Green Lake. Each of the "inmates" is required to dig a hole five feet wide and five feet deep every day. The inmates are also required to report anything interesting they might find as they are digging. Stanley makes friends with another inmate, nicknamed Zero, when he teaches him how to read. Read on to find out what happens when the boys try to escape from Camp Green Lake.

Materials

▶ *Holes* by Louis Sachar
▶ Pencil or pen

Comprehension Questions

Answer the following questions using complete sentences.

1. What choice does the judge give Stanley? Is this fair? Why or why not?

   _____

   _____

2. Why does Stanley lie about stealing the sneakers?

   _____

3. What reason does Mr. Pendanski give the boys for digging holes every day?

   _____

4. When Stanley writes to his mother, why does he lie about Camp Green Lake?

   _____

   _____

5. How does giving X-ray his second "find" affect Stanley's status with the boys?

   _____

   _____

6. When Stanley steals the sunflower seeds, what does the Warden do? Is this fair? Explain your answer. _____

   _____

7. In the end, what does Mr. Sir reveal to Stanley about his guilt? _____

   _____

Famous Quotations

 Read the quotations below. Choose one or more and write what you think they mean on a sheet of notebook paper or in your journal. Then give some examples of ways that you can demonstrate fairness each day.

It isn't necessary to blow out the other person's light in order to let your own shine.
— Anonymous

Injustice anywhere is a threat to justice everywhere. — Martin Luther King, Jr.

Every American ought to have the right to be treated as he would wish to be treated, as one would wish his children to be treated. — John F. Kennedy

Two wrongs will not make one right. — Anonymous

Justice cannot be for one side alone, but must be for both. — Eleanor Roosevelt

We hold these truths to be self-evident, that all men are created equal . . .
— Thomas Jefferson

Justice knows no friendship. — Proverb

No man is above the law and no man below it. — Theodore Roosevelt

Thou shouldst not decide until thou hast heard what both have to say. — Aristophanes

Those who deny freedom to others deserve it not for themselves. — Abraham Lincoln

Don't judge a book by its cover. — Proverb

The only way to have a friend is to be one. — Ralph Waldo Emerson

There are two tellings to every story. — Proverb

Camp Green Lake

Create a brochure to advertise Camp Green Lake.

Pretend that Camp Green Lake from the book *Holes* is a real camp. The people in charge of the camp want to advertise. As you create your brochure, remember what the camp is like. Your brochure can be humorous, serious, or persuasive.

Decide what your purpose is in creating your brochure. Do you want to persuade judges to send boys to Camp Green Lake? Would you rather write the brochure for parents and children to let them know what to expect if they are sentenced to Camp Green Lake? Or do you want to make your brochure a satire of a real summer camp?

Before starting your brochure, you may want to look at several sample brochures from parks, camps, recreation centers, or hotels. Include information in your brochure about the location, activities, and skills that campers will learn. You may also want to include any special features of Camp Green Lake. Your brochure should be informative and colorful.

Materials

- A copy of the book *Holes* by Louis Sachar
- 12" x 18" (30 cm x 46 cm) white card stock or lightweight tagboard
- Assorted colored sheets of construction paper
- Colored pencils or markers
- Ruler
- Scissors
- School glue
- Variety of magazines for pictures
- Travel brochures for pictures

Directions

1. Take one piece of card stock or tagboard. Turn it horizontally so that it is longer from left to right than top to bottom.

2. Fold the tagboard evenly in thirds.

3. Use notebook paper to plan the layout of your brochure. Draw and/or cut out pictures to use in the brochure, and write captions for them.

4. Arrange your writing, pictures, and/or drawings to make your brochure interesting, eye-catching, and colorful.

Read the passage about Elizabeth Blackwell, the first American woman doctor. Read silently or take turns reading aloud in your group. Then work with your group to answer the discussion questions below.

Elizabeth Blackwell was born in England on February 3, 1821. She and her family moved to the United States in 1832. As a young girl, Elizabeth was stubborn and strong-willed, unlike many girls at the time who were reserved and submissive. Little did Elizabeth know that one day she would make history by becoming the first American woman doctor. Elizabeth did not even think about studying medicine until a friend who was dying gave her the idea. Elizabeth had been spending many hours taking care of her sick neighbor. The neighbor commented that she would have been spared some of her suffering had Elizabeth been her doctor.

No American woman had ever attempted to become a doctor before. Medical schools at that time only admitted men. With the help of some sympathetic doctors, Elizabeth spent several years studying medicine before she started applying to medical schools at the age of 25. Although she received 28 rejection letters, Elizabeth did not give up. Finally, the Geneva Medical College in New York sent her an acceptance letter. Upon arriving at the school, Elizabeth learned that the faculty members did not actually want her there. They had allowed the male students to make the choice, and they had voted unanimously to allow her admittance. They had thought it was a practical joke, but the joke was on them. At the end of the two-year program, Doctor Elizabeth Blackwell graduated first in her class.

1. Do you think Elizabeth was treated fairly by the medical schools to which she applied? Explain.

_____

2. Do you think Elizabeth was treated fairly by the Geneva Medical College? Explain.

_____

3. Once Elizabeth became a doctor, do you think she had any more problems with being treated fairly? Explain.

_____

Bulletin Board Set

 Use this bulletin board idea to reinforce the concept of fairness in your classroom. Enlarge the pieces below and glue them onto colorful sheets of construction paper, card stock, or poster board. Have students make additional triangles and then write their own examples of what's fair and what's unfair on them. Arrange the pieces to create a colorful display.

Materials

- Bulletin board pieces below
- Markers, pens, or colored pencils
- Construction paper, card stock, or poster board
- Scissors
- School glue
- Pushpins or stapler

Fair

Listen to both sides of a story.

Follow the rules at home and at school.

Treat others like you would want to be treated.

Avoid gossip or putting other people down.

Unfair

Listen to only one side of a story.

Disrespect those who do not agree with you.

Treat people differently based on their race, religion, or gender.

Gossip and talk about other people when they are not around.

What Is Courage?

Courage . . . is the ability to face your fears with determination and confidence. It is the state of being brave, unafraid, and fearless. It takes courage to admit to others when you have made a mistake. Confronting pain, danger, and trouble are all examples of courage.

Courage is like a muscle; it is strengthened by use.
— Ruth Gordon

It takes courage to grow up and turn out to be who you really are.
— e. e. cummings

Steps to follow to show courage:

❱ Face and deal with trouble, pain, or danger.

❱ Face up to and overcome your fears.

❱ Deal positively with daily difficulties.

❱ Choose to do the right thing over the wrong thing.

❱ Tell the truth in spite of the consequences.

❱ Try new things.

❱ Admit your mistakes and learn from them.

❱ Act bravely even at times when you don't feel brave at all.

Citizenship • Perseverance • **Courage** • Fairness • Honesty • Responsibility • Respect • Kindness • Self-Discipline

Inspire your students to act with courage. Enlarge, decorate, and display this poster in your classroom or copy it and make a transparency to use with your class. Ask students to complete numbers 1 and 2 on the Poster Follow-up activity (page 61), then discuss the poster as a class.

Poster Follow-up

Courage

 Study the "Some Courageous People" poster. Then work in groups of three or four to complete the activity below.

1. In your group, research one of the people named on the poster. Use a variety of sources such as the Internet, encyclopedias, or biographies to find factual information on your assigned person. List the courageous acts that your assigned person has done. Share the information you found with the rest of the class.

_____

_____

_____

_____

_____

2. Do you agree or disagree that each of the people listed on the poster showed courage? Are these really courageous people? Why or why not? Defend your answers.

_____

_____

_____

_____

_____

3. List any other courageous people that you believe should be on a poster.

_____

_____

_____

_____

4. Create your own Courageous People poster using the people you listed in number 3. Sketch what your poster would look on the back of this page. Then create your poster.

Brainstorming

 Close your eyes and think about the word *courage*. What other words come to mind? If you are stumped, try filling in the blank: "Someone who shows courage is _____." Add your responses to the diagram below. A few words have been given to help you get started.

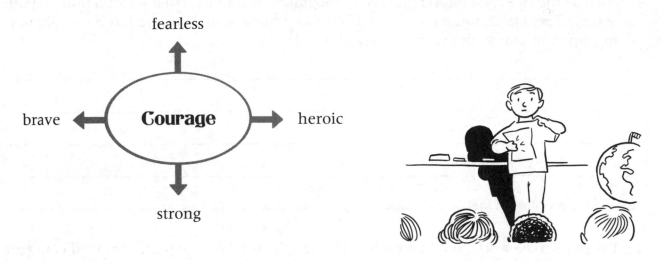

Look at the words in your diagram. How do they relate to things you have done over the last week or two? On the lines below, try to list three situations in which you showed courage. Then list three situations in which you did NOT show courage. Explain what you could have done differently to be more courageous.

Showed courage	Did NOT show courage
1. _____	1. _____
2. _____	2. _____
3. _____	3. _____

Literature Connection

Read *The Sign of the Beaver* by Elizabeth Speare as a class project. In the story, the main character Matt and his father build a home in the wilderness of Maine. When Matt's father returns to Massachusetts to help bring the rest of the family to their new home, Matt is left to guard the new cabin and face the wilderness alone. Matt is saved from drowning by an old Indian and his grandson Attean. Soon Matt and Attean become friends. While Attean teaches Matt survival skills, Matt teaches his friend the English language. Read on to find out what happens to Matt and Attean.

Materials

▶ *The Sign of the Beaver* by Elizabeth George Speare
▶ Pencil or pen

Keeping a Diary

Pretend you are Matt alone in the wilderness. Keep a diary for one week. Include any problems that you face, foods that you eat, fears that you have, and things that you learn while living in the wilderness. Use the space below and additional paper as needed.

Famous Quotations

 Read the quotations below. Choose one or more and write what you think they mean on a sheet of notebook paper or in your journal. Then give some examples of ways that you can show courage each day.

Keep your fears to yourself, but share your courage with others.
— Robert Louis Stevenson

Courage conquers all things. — Ovid

Courage is resistance to fear, mastery of fear—not absence of fear.
— Mark Twain

Courage is being scared to death . . . and saddling up anyway. — John Wayne

Courage is the ladder on which all the other virtues mount. — Clare Boothe Luce

A journey of a thousand miles begins with a single step. — Lao-tzu

To win you have to risk loss. — Jean-Claude Killy

A hero is no braver than an ordinary man, but he is brave five minutes longer.
— Ralph Waldo Emerson

What would life be if we had no courage to attempt anything?
— Vincent van Gogh

The ultimate measure of a person is not where they stand in moments of comfort and convenience, but where they stand at times of challenge and controversy.
— Martin Luther King, Jr.

Critical Thinking

 Read the passage about Harriet Tubman, an abolitionist who was nicknamed "Moses." Read silently or take turns reading aloud in your group. Then work with your group to answer the discussion questions below.

Harriet Ross was born into slavery around 1819 or 1820. Both of her parents were slaves, and she was raised under extremely harsh conditions in Dorchester County, Maryland. When she was about 12, Harriet was seriously injured by a blow to the head. A white overseer threw a weight at a field hand, and Harriet tried to stop him. The weight hit her instead. Harriet suffered from blackouts for the rest of her life because of the injury.

Harriet married a free man, John Tubman, in her mid-twenties. Five years later, after the death of her master, Harriet escaped to Philadelphia because she feared that she would be sold deeper into the South. Members of the Underground Railroad helped Harriet to freedom.

In 1851, Harriet began working with the Underground Railroad to free members of her family. It is believed that Harriet helped approximately 300 people to freedom on the Underground Railroad. She was very spiritual and believed that God would guide her and her charges to freedom. She had strict rules for the people that she helped. Her determination, confidence, and courage inspired those that she led to the North.

Harriet did all of this in spite of the extreme dangers that she faced in returning to the slave states. She worked for the Union as a cook, a nurse, and a spy. At one time there was a $40,000 reward offered for her capture. Harriet Tubman was an extremely courageous woman.

1. Despite the fact that Harriet Tubman escaped from slavery herself, she returned to the slave states to help others. Why do you think Harriet did this?

    _____

    _____

2. What types of dangers did Harriet Tubman face in her lifetime? In what ways did she demonstrate courage? Explain.

    _____

    _____

Role-Playing

 Teacher: Divide the class into small groups. Copy and cut apart the role-playing situations below and have each group select a situation to act out. Give the groups 10 minutes to discuss and prepare their presentations.

Following each group's presentation, have the rest of the class describe ways in which the characters could have demonstrated courage. After the class discussion, have the groups incorporate their classmates' suggestions to reenact their situations, this time demonstrating courage.

Sonya and Marianna, your best friends, want you to smoke with them. You know that it is wrong, but they are your friends and are really persistent.	Mrs. Rodriguez, your choir teacher, wants you to sing a solo for the school assembly in two weeks.
Jimmy and Todd want you, the new kid in class, to water-ski with them. You have never water-skied before and you don't know how to swim very well.	The school bully is picking on someone who is quiet and shy and does not have many friends. You walk up on the situation, and no one else is around.
Mr. Jeffers, your English teacher, wants to talk to you about your test grades after you fail a test for which you did not study.	You arrive home from school and find some freshly baked cookies. You are really hungry, but you know that the cookies are for a party your mom is going to tonight.
While at the movies, you see a friend of yours pick up a wallet that an older neighbor lady has dropped. Your friend does not give the wallet back to the lady.	You borrow your sister's sweater and accidentally snag it on a hook. No one else is home.
Mr. McCurdy knows that you do not like to speak in front of the class, but he wants you to read your poem to the class because it has won an award.	Your friend asks you to lie to his parents and say that he was at your house after school. You find out later that your friend was really buying drugs.

Use this bulletin board idea to reinforce the concept of courage in your classroom. Enlarge and color the pieces below, then glue them onto colorful sheets of construction paper, card stock, or poster board. Have students add their own examples of courageous acts to the set. Arrange the pieces to create a colorful display.

Materials

▸ Bulletin board pieces below

▸ Markers, pens, or colored pencils

▸ Construction paper, card stock, or poster board

▸ Scissors

▸ School glue

▸ Pushpins or stapler

Stand up to a bully.

Confess your mistakes.

Refuse to give in to negative peer pressure.

Try something that you didn't think you could do.

What Is Perseverance?

Perseverance . . . is the act or quality of holding to a course of action, belief, or purpose. To persist or act in spite of opposition or discouragement is to persevere. Sticking to a purpose or a goal and never giving up is another way to express the meaning of the word perseverance. To try and try again, no matter what obstacles are placed before you, demonstrates perseverance. When you stick with an activity regardless of its length or difficulty, you are showing perseverance.

Great works are performed not by strength but by perseverance. — Samuel Johnson

Step after step the ladder is ascended. — Proverb

Steps to follow to show perseverance:

▶ Always do your best and strive for excellence.

▶ Stick with an activity until it is finished.

▶ Complete your assignments even if they are difficult.

▶ Be willing to make a continuing, patient effort.

▶ Set goals and stay focused.

▶ Learn from your mistakes and failures.

▶ Become self-disciplined.

▶ Learn from people who have made it a habit to persevere.

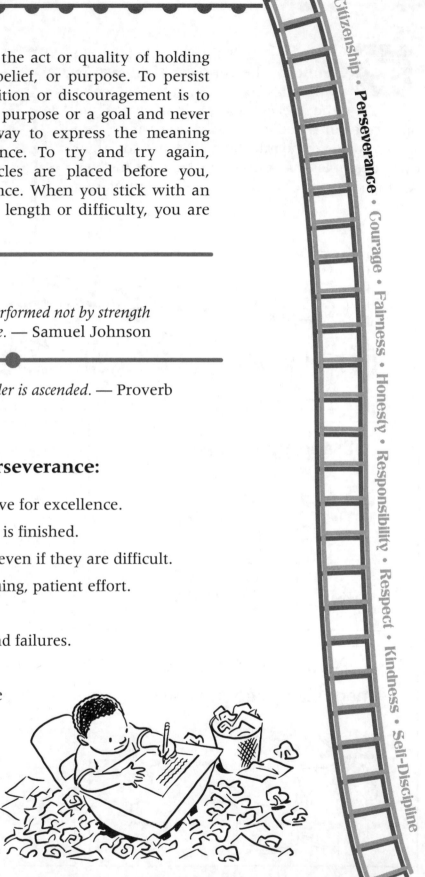

Citizenship • Perseverance • Courage • Fairness • Honesty • Responsibility • Respect • Kindness • Self-Discipline

Inspiration Poster

Inspire your students to practice perseverance. Enlarge, decorate, and display this poster in your classroom or copy it and make a transparency to use with your class. Ask students to write phrases related to perseverance (e.g., "Try your best") on the stars.

Exploring Perseverance

Read each situation below. Do the students demonstrate perseverance? On the lines provided, explain how the students are showing perseverance. If they do not, explain what they could do to show more diligence.

1. Jamie has been working on his social studies project for two weeks. He has only one week left and has completely lost interest.

   _____

   _____

2. Marissa's mother asks her to clean her room to get ready for her slumber party this weekend. Instead of cleaning her room, Marissa talks on the phone with her friends, watches television, and plays computer games.

   _____

   _____

3. Tyra and Anita both want to try out for the softball team. Tyra practices catching and pitching every day with her father and brother. Anita practices only once before tryouts.

   _____

   _____

4. Eduardo's little brother is ill. Eduardo's mother asks him to watch his brother while she goes to the grocery store. Eduardo agrees, but is worried about finishing his essay for English class tomorrow.

   _____

   _____

5. Science is Jason's worst subject. Mrs. Slaton, the science teacher, offers extra help in the mornings before school. Jason arrives at school 30 minutes early each day for two weeks. On the next progress report, Jason's science grade has greatly improved.

   _____

   _____

Brainstorming

 Close your eyes and think about the word *perseverance*. What other words come to mind? If you are stumped, try filling in the blank: "Someone who shows perseverance is _____." Add your responses to the diagram below. A few words have been given to help you get started.

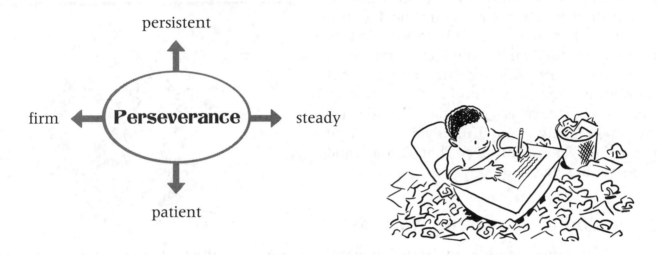

persistent

firm ← **Perseverance** → steady

patient

Look at the words in your diagram. How do they relate to things you have done over the last week or two? On the lines below, try to list three situations in which you showed perseverance. Then list three situations in which you did NOT show perseverance. Explain what you could have done differently to be more resolute.

Showed perseverance	**Did NOT show perseverance**
1. _____	1. _____
_____	_____
_____	_____
2. _____	2. _____
_____	_____
_____	_____
3. _____	3. _____
_____	_____
_____	_____

Literature Connection

Read *From the Mixed-up Files of Mrs. Basil E. Frankweiler* by E. L. Konigsburg. Have you ever thought about running away from home? In this book, Claudia and her little brother Jamie do just that. Claudia knows where she wants to go, but there is just one problem: she does not have enough money. But her little brother does have money. So Claudia convinces Jamie to go on this adventure with her. Their destination is the Metropolitan Museum of Art in New York City. This, of course, is a great place to hide out! They have many wonderful adventures. Read on to discover the mystery that Claudia and Jamie try to solve.

Materials

▶ *From the Mixed-up Files of Mrs. Basil E. Frankweiler* by E. L. Konigsburg

▶ Pencil or pen

If You Could Change the World . . .

In the story, Jamie becomes interested in learning more about the time in which Michelangelo lived. This time period is known as the Renaissance. During this time, many discoveries in medicine and science were made. Numerous artists created beautiful statues, architecture, and paintings. If you could change the world today and make it a better place, what do you suppose you would do? Choose one positive change that you would make and draw a picture or write a paragraph about that change in the space below.

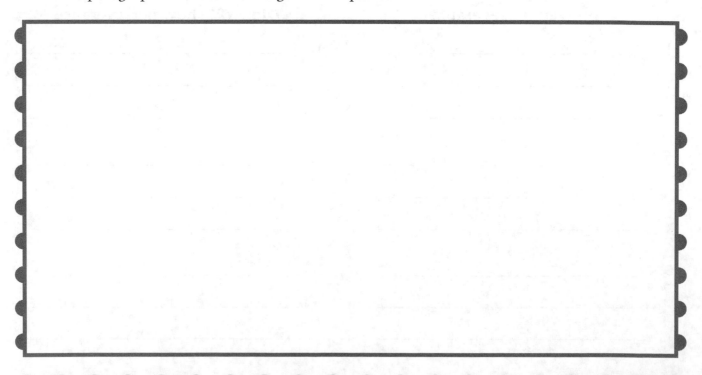

Famous Quotations

Read the quotations below. Choose one or more and write what you think they mean on a sheet of notebook paper or in your journal. Then give some examples of ways that you can show perseverance each day.

The strength of the bee is its persistence. — Anonymous

The difference between the impossible and the possible lies in a man's determination. — Tommy Lasorda

Little strokes fell great oaks. — Benjamin Franklin

Most of the important things in the world have been accomplished by people who have kept on trying when there seemed to be no hope at all. — Dale Carnegie

I never failed once. I invented the light bulb. It just happened to be a 2,000-step process. — Thomas Edison

He who perseveres will succeed. — Anonymous

Energy and persistence conquer all things. — Benjamin Franklin

We must have perseverance and above all confidence in ourselves. — Marie Curie

Success consists of getting up just one more time than you fall. — Oliver Goldsmith

He who labors incessantly attains success easily. — Anonymous

Through perseverance, many people win success out of what seemed destined to be certain failure. — Benjamin Disraeli

Consider the postage stamp, my son. It secures success through its ability to stick to one thing till it gets there. — Josh Billings

Critical Thinking

Read the passage about Thomas Edison, who was both an inventor and a scientist. Read silently or take turns reading aloud in your group. Then work with your group to answer the discussion questions below.

Thomas Edison, born in 1847 in Milan, Ohio, was one of the greatest inventors the world has ever known. In his lifetime, Edison patented 1,093 inventions. Because of his numerous inventions, he acquired the nickname "The Wizard of Menlo Park." Inventing was so important to Edison that he even left his job as a telegraph operator to devote his life to inventing.

As a child, Thomas was extremely curious. He wanted to know how things worked. If he did not know, he would ask many questions. When he was eight years old, he became bored with memorizing and repeating facts, which was the method of schooling at that time. The teacher thought he asked too many questions and said that he was "addled." Edison's mother disagreed and began to teach him at home.

In 1877, Edison invented the lightbulb. However, he searched for two more years to find the correct material to make the light glow. He experimented with many materials, including his own hair, straw, horsehair, and coconut hair. Edison was determined to succeed. If an experiment was unsuccessful, he did not see it as a failure, but rather as a learning experience.

Finally, after more than a thousand experiments, Edison's perseverance paid off in 1879, when he invented carbonized thread to place inside the lightbulb. Thomas Edison thus led the way to the age of electricity and changed the world forever. The world became a better and safer place because of this new way to light up a dark room or a street.

1. What do you think allowed Thomas Edison to persevere even though he had many failures? Explain.

_____

_____

2. Thomas Edison set many goals and proved that through his perseverance he was able to accomplish those goals. Choose a goal for yourself and develop a plan that will enable you to reach that goal.

_____

_____

Poetry Connection

 Work with a partner and take turns reading the poems on perseverance. After reading the two poems, make a Venn diagram comparing and contrasting how the character trait of perseverance is portrayed in each one.

Believing in Yourself

There may be days
when you get up in the morning
and things aren't the way
you had hoped they would be.
That's when you have to tell yourself
that things will get better.

There are times when people
disappoint you and let you down,
but those are the times
when you must remind yourself
to keep life focused on believing in
yourself and all that you are capable of.

There will be challenges to face
and changes to make in your life,
and it is up to you to accept them.
Constantly keep yourself headed
in the right direction.
It may not be easy at times,
but in those times of struggle you will
find a stronger sense of who you are.

So when the days come
that are filled with frustration
and unexpected responsibilities,
remember to believe in yourself
and all you want your life to be,
because the challenges and changes
will only help you to find the goals
that you know are meant
to come true for you.

— Anonymous

Meanings

Standing for what you believe in,
regardless of the odds against you,
and the pressure that tears at your resistance,
  . . . means courage.

Keeping a smile on your face,
when inside you feel like dying,
for the sake of supporting others,
  . . . means strength.

Doing more than is expected,
to make another's life a little more bearable,
without uttering a single complaint,
  . . . means compassion.

Helping a friend in need,
no matter the time or the effort,
to the best of your ability,
  . . . means loyalty.

Giving more than you have,
and expecting nothing,
but nothing in return,
  . . . means selflessness.

Holding your head high,
and being the best you know you can be,
when life seems to fall apart at your feet,
facing each difficulty with the confidence
that time will bring you better tomorrows,
and never giving up,
  . . . means confidence.

— Anonymous

CD-0072 *Character Education*

Use this bulletin board idea to reinforce the concept of perseverance in your classroom. Enlarge and color the pieces below, then glue them onto colorful sheets of construction paper, card stock, or poster board. Make enough copies so there is one path for each student. Have students set goals for themselves (e.g., "Make the soccer team" or "Earn A's on all of my tests"). Have them write their names above the paths and their goals beneath the finish lines. Arrange the pieces to create a colorful display.

Materials

- Bulletin board pieces below
- Markers, pens, or colored pencils
- Construction paper, card stock, or poster board
- Scissors
- School glue
- Pushpins or stapler

What Is Citizenship?

Citizenship . . . means doing your best to make your home, community, neighborhood, and school better places. A good citizen obeys rules and respects authority. In a democratic society, independence and freedom are treasured. As a good citizen, it is your duty and obligation to do your share to improve and honor these traditions.

What we would do if we were president is not half as important as what we will do as plain citizens. — Anonymous

Ask not what your country can do for you; ask what you can do for your country. — John F. Kennedy

Steps to follow to show good citizenship:

▶ Know and care about your community and country.

▶ Understand that with every right there comes a responsibility.

▶ Obey laws and rules, and respect authority.

▶ Use kind words and demonstrate good manners.

▶ Accept responsibility for your actions.

▶ Participate and become involved by making contributions to your community.

▶ Be a good neighbor.

▶ Show concern for the needs of others.

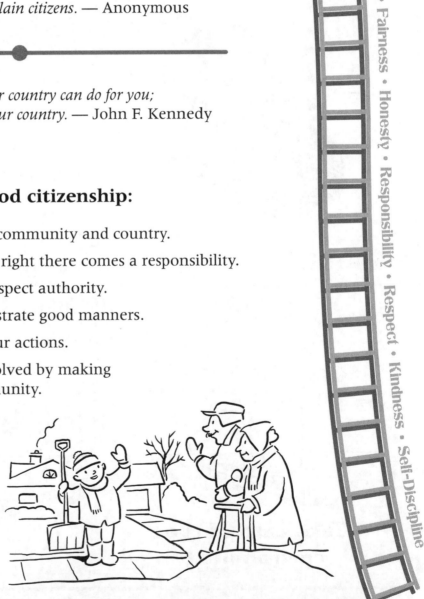

Inspire your students to practice good citizenship. Enlarge, decorate, and display this poster in your classroom or copy it and make a transparency to use with your class. Ask students to name other things they can do to be good citizens.

Be a Good Citizen by Offering a Helping Hand

Obey rules

Vote and take action

Take care of the environment

Help others

What Makes a Good Citizen?

Name _____

Read each of the following situations. Decide if a good citizen would behave in the manner described. If so, circle YES. If not, circle NO. Explain your answer on the line provided.

1. Jeremy is working with a group in class. After a while, he takes control and tells everyone else what to do. Jeremy, however, sits back and does nothing.

   YES   NO

   _____

2. Alex borrowed Merinda's newest book and accidentally spilled juice on it. He apologizes and offers to pay Merinda for the book.

   YES   NO

   _____

3. As Mrs. Clark was walking down the hallway at school, she noticed several pieces of trash scattered along the floor. She stopped to pick up the trash and threw it in the nearest trash can.

   YES   NO

   _____

4. A new school has just opened. Students have been asked to vote on a mascot for the school. Keri says that she is too busy and does not vote. When the new mascot is chosen, Keri complains that she does not like it.

   YES   NO

   _____

5. The school's 4-H Club is working on a service project to clean up trash along the main highway near the school. Angelica asks six students to help her with the project. Together they collect 14 bags full of trash.

   YES   NO

   _____

Brainstorming

 Close your eyes and think about the word *citizenship*. What other words come to mind? If you are stumped, try filling in the blank: "A good citizen is _____." Add your responses to the diagram below. A few words have been given to help you get started.

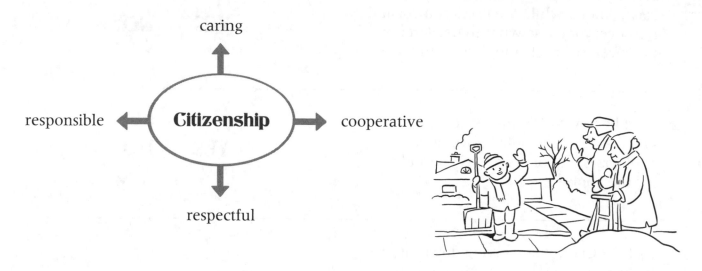

caring

responsible ← **Citizenship** → cooperative

respectful

Look at the words in your diagram. How do they relate to things you have done over the last week or two? On the lines below, try to list three situations in which you acted like a good citizen. Then list three situations in which you did NOT act like a good citizen. Explain what you could have done differently to be a better citizen.

Acted like a good citizen	**Did NOT act like a good citizen**
1. _____	1. _____
_____	_____
_____	_____
2. _____	2. _____
_____	_____
_____	_____
3. _____	3. _____
_____	_____
_____	_____

Literature Connection

 Read *The Giver* by Lois Lowry and learn that the way we wish life to be may not be the best way after all. Jonas lives sometime in the future in a nameless community. There is no war, poverty, hate, pollution, or disease. There is also no choice, color, music, or love. Jonas is anxious to learn what his lifetime profession will be. He is selected to be the next Receiver of Memories. He soon discovers that he wants more and wishes everyone could feel love and pain. Read on to discover the cliff-hanger ending.

> ## Materials
> ▶ *The Giver* by Lois Lowry
> ▶ Pencil or pen

Comprehension Questions

Answer the questions using complete sentences.

1. Everyone in the community must follow rules. List at least five of these rules.

   _____

   _____

   _____

   _____

   _____

2. "Nines" receive an important object at their Ceremony. What is it and what does it mean?

   _____

   _____

3. Why are the people in the community being protected from having to make choices?

   _____

   _____

4. Jonas doesn't want to play the "good guys/bad guys" game anymore. Why not?

   _____

   _____

5. What things does the Giver transmit to Jonas to help him on his journey?

   _____

   _____

Famous Quotations

Read the quotations below. Choose one or more and write what you think they mean on a sheet of notebook paper or in your journal. Then give some examples of ways that you can be a good citizen each day.

Every good citizen makes his country's honor his own, and cherishes it not only as precious but as sacred. — Andrew Jackson

If men were angels, no government would be necessary. — James Madison

When you have decided what you believe, what you feel must be done, have the courage to stand alone and be counted. — Eleanor Roosevelt

If everyone swept in front of his house, the whole town would be clean. — Anonymous

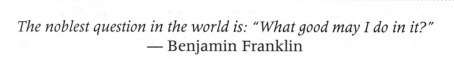

The noblest question in the world is: "What good may I do in it?" — Benjamin Franklin

If you have no will to change it, you have no right to criticize it. — Anonymous

You are on the pathway to a successful life when you do more for the community than the community does for you. — Anonymous

Actions speak louder than words. — Proverb

To protect those who are not able to protect themselves is a duty which every one owes to society. — Edward Macnaghten

Life is not so short but that there is always time enough for courtesy. — Ralph Waldo Emerson

Critical Thinking

 Read the passage about Sandra Day O'Connor, the first woman ever to serve as a U.S. Supreme Court justice. Read silently or take turns reading aloud in your group. Then work with your group to answer the discussion questions below.

Being the first at something is not always easy. Perhaps you were the first person in your family to learn how to use a computer, how to play a piano, or how to snowboard. The first person to do something needs to be able to face all the responsibilities and difficulties that go with it. Such a person was Sandra Day O'Connor, the first woman ever to be appointed to the United States Supreme Court in 1981. The U.S. Supreme Court is the highest court in the nation. Its job is to interpret the U.S. Constitution.

Mrs. O'Connor became a lawyer in the early 1950s and applied to work for law firms in both San Francisco and Los Angeles. They rejected her because she was a woman. Even though she was very smart, it did not matter. People in the legal world were not accustomed to having women in the courtroom. Mrs. O'Connor found that the government was more accepting of women. She took a job as a deputy county attorney in California. For a short time she and a partner had their own law practice. In 1965, she served as assistant attorney general for the state of Arizona. Between 1969 and 1974, she served as an Arizona state senator. Then, in 1974, she ran for and was elected a superior court judge. Finally, in 1981, President Ronald Reagan nominated Mrs. O'Connor to be the first woman Supreme Court justice.

Sandra Day O'Connor is so much more than the first U.S. Supreme Court justice. She is a wife, a mother, a grandmother, a citizen, and a wonderful role model for women. Justice O'Connor has said, "Whether your future work is in business, government, or as a volunteer, try to set your sights on doing something worthwhile and then work hard at it."

1. List some ways that Mrs. O'Connor demonstrated citizenship. _____

_____

_____

2. Why do you think women were not accepted in the legal world at first? Explain.

_____

_____

Citizen Participation

There are many citizens who do not participate in our government. These people do not vote, sign petitions, write letters to their representatives, protest things that they think are unfair, serve as jurors, or run for any office. Then there are other people who believe that citizens have a responsibility to participate in government. If you do decide to participate in government, you will need to think about how much time you are willing to commit. Read and answer the following questions.

1. Do you feel that you are a good citizen? Explain your answer.

   _____

   _____

   _____

2. Do citizens have a responsibility to work to improve society? Why or why not?

   _____

   _____

   _____

3. Should citizens be concerned with improving the lives of those who are less fortunate? Why or why not?

   _____

   _____

   _____

4. If you do not choose to vote or participate in government in any way, should you still be required to obey the laws? Why or why not?

   _____

   _____

   _____

Bulletin Board Set

 Use this bulletin board idea to reinforce the concept of good citizenship in your classroom. Enlarge and color the pieces below, then glue them onto colorful sheets of construction paper, card stock, or poster board. Have students add their own text and images to describe what they think makes a good citizen. Arrange the pieces to create a colorful display.

Materials

- Bulletin board pieces below
- Markers, pens, or colored pencils
- Construction paper, card stock, or poster board
- Scissors
- School glue
- Pushpins or stapler

What makes a good citizen?

A good citizen . . .

obeys the laws

shows patriotism

does community service

votes in elections

CD-0072 *Character Education*

You Don't Say! A Mini-Play about Responsibility

This play uses humor to teach students about the importance of responsibility. Review the definition of responsibility as described on page 32. Then assign students to read the different characters' parts. Allow students time to practice and learn their parts. When they're ready, have students perform the play for the class. Invite parents and/or other classes to the performance if you wish. Use the follow-up questions on page 89 to discuss aspects of the play after the performance.

Characters in order of appearance:

Jessica
Andrew
Matt
Jerry Atrics (Grandfather)

Mrs. Moody
Adrienne's mother
Adrienne

As the play begins, there are two phones on the stage—one on a desk in the den, the other in the hallway near the den. Sound effects for the phone may be used from off-stage. The phone rings and Jessica enters.

Jessica .... Hello? Oh, hi. How are you, Connie? *(Pause)* You don't say! *(Pause)* Adrienne didn't do her what? *(Pause)* Social studies project? *(Pause)* Doesn't she know she'll get a ZERO? *(Pause)* She doesn't want her parents to know because she still wants to go to Six Flags this weekend? Oh, I see. Adrienne's afraid her parents will ground her for the rest of her life. I have to go and call Andrew.

(The phone rings. Andrew enters and answers.)

Andrew .... Helloooooo?

Jessica .... Andrew, this is Jessica!

Andrew .... You don't say!

Jessica .... You'll never believe what happened. Adrienne didn't do her social studies project. Mrs. Eubanks is giving her a ZERO! Now she won't be able to go to Six Flags ever again!

Andrew .... You don't say! I need to call Matt and let him know.

(Andrew calls Matt. The phone rings. Matt enters and answers the phone.)

Matt .... Hi there!

Andrew .... Matt, you won't believe what happened! Adrienne didn't do her social studies project, and Mrs. Eubanks may kick her out of school. Her parents won't let her go to Six Flags or anywhere, not even to buy new clothes.

Matt .... You don't say! Now what am I going to do? We were supposed to go to Six Flags together. I guess I'll call my grandfather to see if I can go to his house on Saturday. Okay, good-bye.

(Matt phones his grandfather. The phone rings. Grandfather enters and answers the phone.)

Grandfather .... Hello, who is this?

Matt .... *(Speaking loudly because his grandfather is hard of hearing)* Grandfather, it's me, Matt!

Grandfather .... Who? Rat who?

Matt .... Not Rat! Matt, your grandson!

Grandfather .... Oh, Matt! How are you?

Matt .... Fine, Grandfather. Could I come over and visit you this weekend? My friend Adrienne didn't do her social studies project. She's getting kicked out of school, and she can't go to Six Flags or anywhere!

Grandfather .... You don't say! Sure, you can come over and help me pick up sticks and trash in the yard. I'll see you then, Matt!

(Matt exits. Grandfather calls Mrs. Moody. The phone rings. Mrs. Moody answers.)

Mrs. Moody .... The Moody residence.

Grandfather .... Hello, Mrs. Moody. This is Jerry Atrics, Matt's grandfather. Tell your daughter Connie that she doesn't need to come help me with the yard this weekend. My grandson Matt is going to help me instead.

Mrs. Moody .... But I thought Matt was going to Six Flags with Adrienne.

Grandfather .... No, Adrienne is being kicked out of school and has to pick up sticks and wear clothes that sag because she didn't turn in her social studies project.

Mrs. Moody .... You don't say! Isn't that a bit harsh? Well, I've got to go. Good-bye.

*(Mrs. Moody hangs up the phone. Grandfather exits.
Mrs. Moody phones Adrienne's mother.
Adrienne's mother enters and answers the phone.)*

Adrienne's mother .... Hello? Who's speaking?

Mrs. Moody .... This is Mrs. Moody. I was just calling to find out what's going on with Adrienne. I hear she's leaving school to go work at Six Flags where she will be picking up sticks and wearing rags. And all this because she didn't turn in her social studies project?

Adrienne's mother .... No daughter of mine will be leaving school to work at Six Flags, picking up sticks and wearing rags. I need to talk to Adrienne! I'll call you later. Good-bye.

(Mrs. Moody exits. Adrienne enters.)

Adrienne .... Hi, Mom. What's up?

Adrienne's mother .... What's this I hear about you quitting school to work at Six Flags, wearing rags and picking up sticks because you didn't turn in your social studies project? Won't Mrs. Eubanks let you turn it in late?

Adrienne .... Yes, I'm turning it in tomorrow. I'll lose some points, though. Mrs. Eubanks said that I was being irresponsible. I need to call Matt about our trip to Six Flags. Can I go now?

Evaluating the Play

 Answer and discuss the questions below after reading or watching a performance of the play, *You Don't Say!*

1. What responsibility did Adrienne have?

   _____

   _____

2. Did she complete her task on time?

   _____

   _____

3. Did Adrienne understand the consequences for not completing her task?

   _____

   _____

4. Do you think Adrienne did her best? Why or why not?

   _____

   _____

5. How did Adrienne's irresponsibility affect other people?

   _____

   _____

6. Do you think Adrienne's mother will allow her to go to Six Flags? Why or why not?

   _____

   _____

7. Did Jessica do the right thing? Why or why not?

   _____

   _____

8. How did Jessica's actions affect others?

   _____

   _____

Character Crossword

Complete the puzzle by choosing the character trait from the list that best fits each clue.

citizenship

courage

fairness

honesty

kindness

perseverance

respect

responsibility

self-discipline

Across

4. _____ is the training and control of one's self and one's conduct.

8. _____ means showing concern for the rights of others and treating them as you would want to be treated.

9. _____ is the ability to face your fears.

Down

1. _____ is being truthful, genuine, sincere, and trustworthy.

2. _____ means being accountable for who you are and what you do.

3. _____ is being generous, friendly, and warm-hearted.

5. _____ means being free of favoritism.

6. _____ is being respectful of the rights, duties, and privileges of all citizens.

7. _____ means sticking to a purpose.

Field Trips and Community Service

The following are suggestions for combining field trips with community service projects to enhance your students' study of character education.

Project #1

Encourage students to demonstrate *kindness* and *citizenship* by planning a field trip to a homeless shelter in your community or city. Before making the trip, work with students to plan how they can help out at the shelter. Could your students volunteer to collect food, hygiene items, blankets, clothing, and/or books? If so, you may want to help students organize a collection drive before the scheduled date of your field trip. Would your students be willing and able to help clean up around the homeless shelter? If so, contact the shelter in advance so you can work together to make arrangements for your students to do volunteer work while they are there.

Project #2

Encourage *citizenship* and *responsibility* in your students by planning a field trip to the governor's, mayor's, or city council's office. Prior to making the trip, ask your students to make a list of questions to ask the governor, mayor, or city council member: *How can we make our state/community/city a better place to live? What do you feel is the most rewarding part of your position as governor/mayor/city council member? What are some of your main responsibilities?* Brainstorm with students before the trip about possible related community service projects they could do. Would they be willing to adopt a street, road, park, or highway in the community and clean it up once a month? Discuss realistic options for projects your class could work together to complete.

Project #3

Foster *kindness, respect, responsibility,* and *citizenship* in your students by planning a field trip to a nursing home or other facility for the elderly in your community. Before making the trip, ask students what they could do to make the visit meaningful for the residents. Could the students prepare and put on a concert or a play? Maybe they could bake treats to take along, or bring puzzles and stories to share with the seniors. You may also want to encourage students to think about what they will talk about with the residents. Possible topics include their jobs, travels, friends, and families.

Bibliography

Use these titles to help reinforce and make connections with your character education program.

Self-Discipline
Dancing Horses by Helen Griffiths
*The Flies and the Honey Pot, The Frogs
    and the Well,* and *The Goose That
    Laid the Golden Eggs* by Aesop
Hatchet by Gary Paulsen
Zan Hagen's Marathon by R. R. Knudson

Kindness
Annie Sullivan by Mary Malone
Charlie and the Chocolate Factory by
    Roald Dahl
The Lion and the Mouse by Aesop
Spring and the Shadow Man by
    Emily Rhoads Johnson

Respect
Frozen Fire: A Tale of Courage by
    James Houston
*The Great Kapok Tree: A Tale of the
    Amazon Rain Forest* by Lynne Cherry
Number the Stars by Lois Lowry
Through Grandpa's Eyes by
    Patricia MacLachlan
The Ugly Duckling by
    Hans Christian Andersen

Responsibility
April Morning by Howard Fast
Dear Mr. Henshaw by Beverly Cleary
A Dog on Barkham Street by Mary Stolz
Last Summer with Maizon by
    Jacqueline Woodson
Shoemaker Martin by Leo Tolstoy

Honesty
The Boy Who Cried Wolf by Aesop
Honestly, Myron by Dean Hughes
A Penny's Worth of Character by
    Jesse Stuart
Pinocchio by Carlo Lorenzini
Shiloh by Phyllis Reynolds Naylor

Fairness
Chicken Sunday by Patricia Polacco
Holes by Louis Sachar
The Secret Grove by Barbara Nash Cohen
Three Gold Pieces: A Greek Folk Tale
    by Aliki
The Watsons Go to Birmingham—1963
    by Christopher Paul Curtis

Courage
Helen Keller by Margaret Davidson
The Night the Monster Came by
    Mary Calhoun
The Sign of the Beaver by
    Elizabeth George Speare
Sixth-Grade Sleepover by Eve Bunting
A Time to Be Brave by Christel Kleitsch
    and Paul Stephens

Perseverance
*From the Mixed-up Files of Mrs. Basil E.
    Frankweiler* by E. L. Konigsburg
How Far, Felipe? by Genevieve Gray
"The Steadfast Tin Soldier" by Hans
    Christian Andersen in *The Book
    of Virtues: A Treasury of Great Moral
    Stories,* edited by William J. Bennett
"Try, Try Again" and "Persevere" in
    The Children's Book of Virtues, edited
    by William J. Bennett
*A Weed Is a Flower: The Life of George
    Washington Carver* by Aliki

Citizenship
Baseball Saved Us by Ken Mochizuki
Frindle by Andrew Clements
The Giver by Lois Lowry
In the Year of the Boar and Jackie Robinson
    by Bette Bao Lord
Marvin Redpost: Class President by
    Louis Sachar

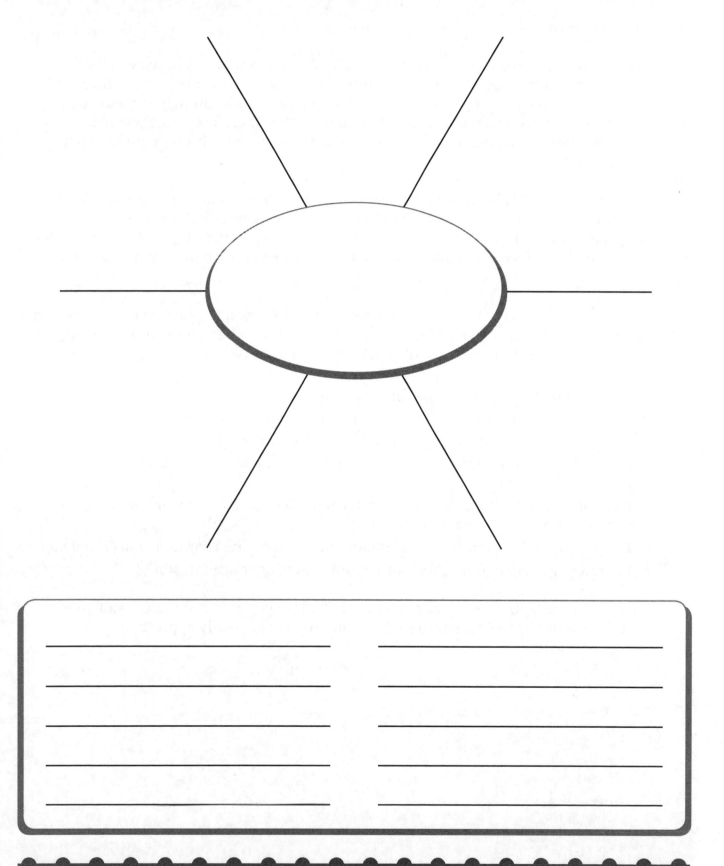

Letter to Parents

Dear Parents/Guardians,

Given the events of the past few years, our school believes that it is now even more important that we work together to prepare our students to become productive citizens of tomorrow. We feel that a strong character based on ethical values can help students make the right decisions when faced with difficult situations. It is, therefore, our hope that you will join us in our efforts to strengthen our school and our community through our character education program.

Our school is involved in an ongoing program that highlights nine key components of character education: self-discipline, kindness, respect, responsibility, honesty, fairness, courage, perseverance, and citizenship. Our class will be participating in a variety of activities. Some of the activities will be completed in class, while others may require your assistance at home.

We'd like to emphasize the fact that you are your child's most important teacher. As such, here are some suggestions for what you can do to support our character education study and, thus, help your child at home, at school, and in our community:

- Make it a point to go over assignments your child brings home.
- Provide a quiet, well-lit area for your child to work.
- Be sure to review the work your child has finished at home.
- Remember: children learn by watching. Set an example of how you want your child to behave.
- If possible, share stories from your own childhood that relate to any of the nine character traits discussed in this book.
- Praise your child when he or she exhibits any of the nine character traits listed above.
- Volunteer to help at our school during our character education study!

Thank you for your time and assistance. Your child is very important to us, and your understanding of our school's character education program is greatly appreciated.

Sincerely,

Award Certificate

presented to

_____
Name

for having completed the
Character Education Study at

_____
School

_____
Signature

_____
Date

Citizenship

Perseverance

Courage

Fairness

Honesty

Responsibility

Respect

Kindness

Self-Discipline

Answer Key

Page 18
1. There is only one person who works in the family and that is Charlie's father.
2. Answers will vary.
3. Grandpa Joe knows all about the factory.
4. His family taught him good manners.
5. Mr. Wonka is going to give Charlie and his family a place to live and keep them fed. He is going to let Charlie take over the factory when he is old enough.

Page 36
1. Leigh used the same book for a report three years in a row. He wants Mrs. Henshaw to give him the answers for his report on an author.
2. He made an alarm for his lunch box. Leigh was given some money by his father which he used to purchase and make the alarm.
3. No. He is late with his support check. He doesn't call Leigh when he says he will. He loses Bandit.
4. The other students saw how well Leigh's alarm worked and made their own alarms.

Page 45
1. Shiloh hadn't been in their yard.
2. He gets hungry before bedtime.
3. There's not much for his friend David to do at their home.
4. He saw a snake up on the hill about 4 feet long.
5. His mother has had a headache lately and can't take any noise so David can't come over.

Page 54
1. Stanley can go to jail, or he can go to Camp Green Lake. (Answers will vary.)
2. He thought the other boys' crimes were worse and that no one would believe he was innocent.
3. Mr. Pendanski says that digging holes helps them to build character.
4. Stanley lies to his mother because he does not want his mother to worry about him.
5. Stanley gets to move up a place in the water line which means he has moved up in their ranks.

6. She gently scrapes Stanley with her poisonous nails and viciously scratches Mr. Sir. This is not fair. (Answers may vary.)
7. He tells Stanley that he is innocent.

Page 81
1. Every family has two children. No bragging is allowed. You must take a pill for "Stirrings." Everyone does volunteer hours. No rudeness is allowed. No bike riding is allowed until "Nines" Ceremony.
2. "Nines" receive a bicycle. It symbolizes moving out into the community and away from the family unit.
3. They are being protected from the pressure and stress of making decisions. Perhaps they are also being protected from the pain of making wrong decisions.
4. It reminds him of the memory of war.
5. He transmits endurance, courage, and strength to Jonas.

Page 89
1. Adrienne was to complete her social studies project.
2. No, she did not.
3. Yes, she knew she would lose points.
4. (Answers will vary.) No, because she did not meet the deadline.
5. (Answers will vary.) Other people had to change their plans.
6. Answers will vary.
7. Answers will vary.

Page 90

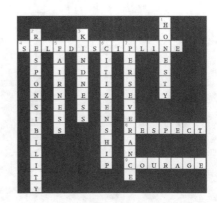